I0478416

EXPERT ADVISOR PROGRAMMING
FOR BEGINNERS

By
Wayne Walker

Table of Contents

1.Basics of trading

1.2 What is trading in financial terms?

Trading is buying or selling an instrument with the aim to profit from the trade. You speculate on the price going up or down. You can either go **long(buy)** where you buy an instrument and attempt to sell it at a higher price. Or you can go **short(sell)** where you borrow an instrument that sells at a high price and you speculate that the price will decrease, when the price has decreased you buy it back from the market and return it to the owner, a market-maker, you keep the decrease in price as profit.

You can trade leveraged or unleveraged. If your leverage is 1:200 that means for every dollar you have in your account, you have the buying power of 200 times. If you have 500 USD in account, you can buy for 200 x 500=10 000 dollars amount of the security. The margin is the amount that you are required to have in your account to use the leverage.

1.3 Different types of market orders

Buy Market order: You buy the instrument at the current spot price.

Buy Limit order: If the current market price is 100, you can place a buy limit order at 95 to buy if the price goes down.

Buy Stop order: If current market price is 100 and you want to buy if it goes above 110 then you place a buy stop order at that level, and it will be triggered if the price goes above it.

You can also do these type of orders on the sell side .ex. sell limit, sell stop, sell market.

1.4 Stop-loss and Take-profit

Sometimes the market moves quickly and if you are unable be in front of your computer it is possible to set exit orders for your trades. These orders are called **stop-loss** and **take-profit**. Stop-loss is an order that is triggered if your trade moves against you and ends with a loss. Take-profit is the opposite, it is how much profit you want from the market.

2 Automatic Trading – Algorithm

2.1 Why automatic trading – why develop algorithm of your trading strategy?

There are several advantages of quantitative trading. People have feelings and emotions attached to their money, they prefer to lose small and win big. Let us imagine you have just executed a trade, what you will experience is that you don't want to close a losing trade, it's difficult to take the loss. However, if you are in profit you will prefer to close your trade with a small profit. What you may also experience is that after closing the winning trade the market continues in your favor. It is difficult emotionally to follow the rule *"cut your losses and let profits run"*. By automating your strategy, you allow your algorithm to do the trading and detach your feelings from the strategy. You have predefined rules in your algorithm which are executed without your interaction.

As humans, it is difficult and time consuming to monitor all the markets and wait for all entry signals. By automating your trading you save time and increase the number of instruments you are able to trade because you run your algorithm on them instead. You can trade whenever you want, whichever market you want, without using so much time in front of the computer.

When you are trying to develop a trading strategy, several ideas come in your head. You start studying charts and look 2-3 months in the past to see how the strategy would have done. That period is not enough, you need to run many years of backtest to prove if a strategy is good. That can only be done by developing an algorithm and do backtesting of several years, on different instruments and timeframes. However, you don't have time to do it manually because it's time consuming and time used for developing a new trading system will decrease. By learning to code you become equipped to develop new trading strategies and you also will be able to detect false ones.

2.2 Progamming language

There are several languages you can use to program your trading strategy. What is true is that there is not much difference between the languages. If you can code one language you can code other languages too, you just need to do some tweaks in how you code, but the basics are similar for many of them.

We will use the Meta Trader 4 platform. They use mql programming which is similar to java/C/C#/C++. The reason we are using this platform are several. It's open source which means it's free to code a strategy, backtest and run it on a demo account. The trading community using this language is huge, so if you any problems you can just google the solution on the internet. You don't have to gather historical data either, it's already on the platform. Finally, many brokers are using the platform so it's not difficult to find a broker with the preferences you require.

The goal of this book is to be hands-on and it will teach you what you need to code your own trading strategy.

3 MetaTrader and MetaEditor

3.1 MetaTrader

MetaTrader is the platform where you trade, you have your charts, run your algorithms, test strategies, basically everything you execute is done on this platform. Here you can also do your manual trading. Everything that you normally can do on a trading platform can you do here.

3-1 Picture above shows the Meta trader.

3.2 MetaEditor

We need to launch our MetaEditor, which is a platform where you create your own indicators, algorithms which are expert advisors or write a script by coding it. You use MetaTrader to execute what you code in MetaEditor.

Open MetaTrader – go to the terminal – click on the "yellow book" – you will then open MetaEditor

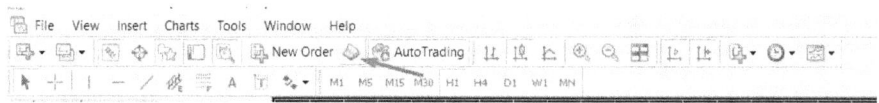

3-2 Above is picture of the toolbar on Metatrader, click on the "yellow book" which is metaEditor.

Short key is: *Alt +F4*

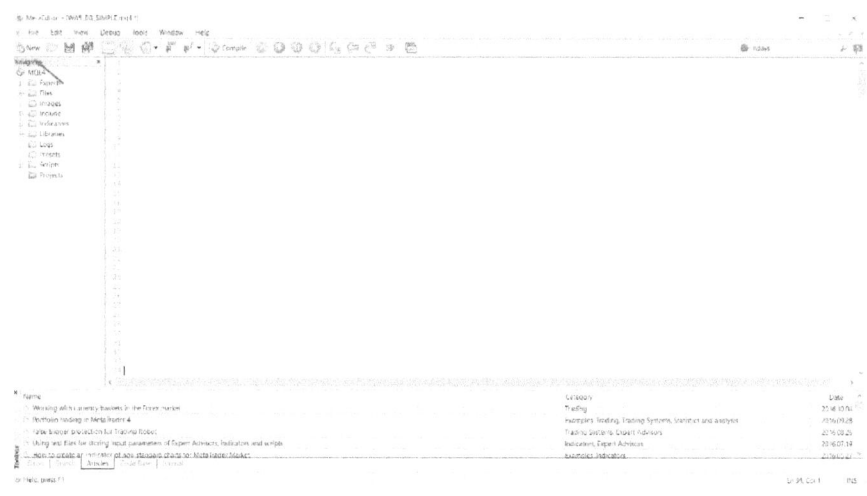

3-3 Picture above shows the MetaEditor.

Picture 3-3 shows MetaEditor, as MetaTrader this also has a toolbar which consist of buttons you frequently use.

3.3 Create new Expert Advisor/Algorithm

At the toolbar to the left you have a button called *New,* click on it.

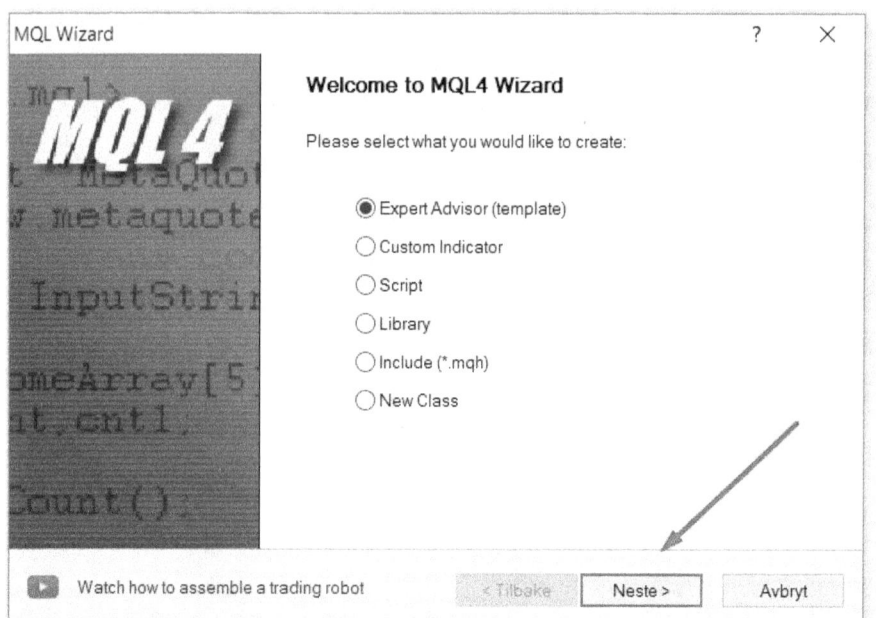

3-4 This box will appear when you click on the new button(næste=next on English platforms).

In this editor, you have an option to develop several scripts which you can run, but what we will use is Expert Advisor which is a trading Algorithm, and we tick off *Expert Advisor(template)* and press *next.* Then a wizard will appear up where you must specify the general properties of your Algorithm.

Name: You write the name of your Algorithm
Author: Who is the owner of this algorithm, write your name here
Link: If you have a website you can paste a link to it here

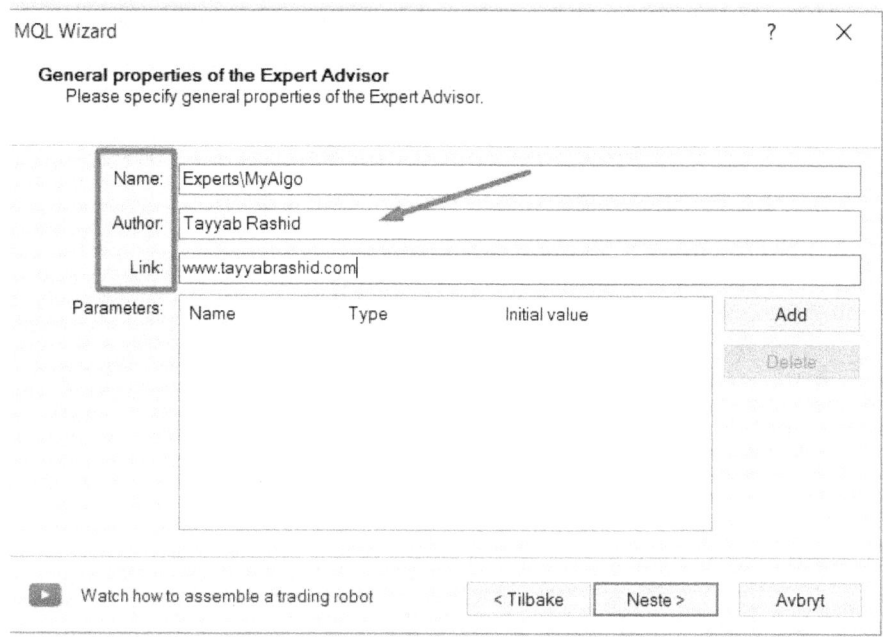

3-5 General properties wizard.

You don't need to fill in anything other than general properties, let everything else remain as is and press next.

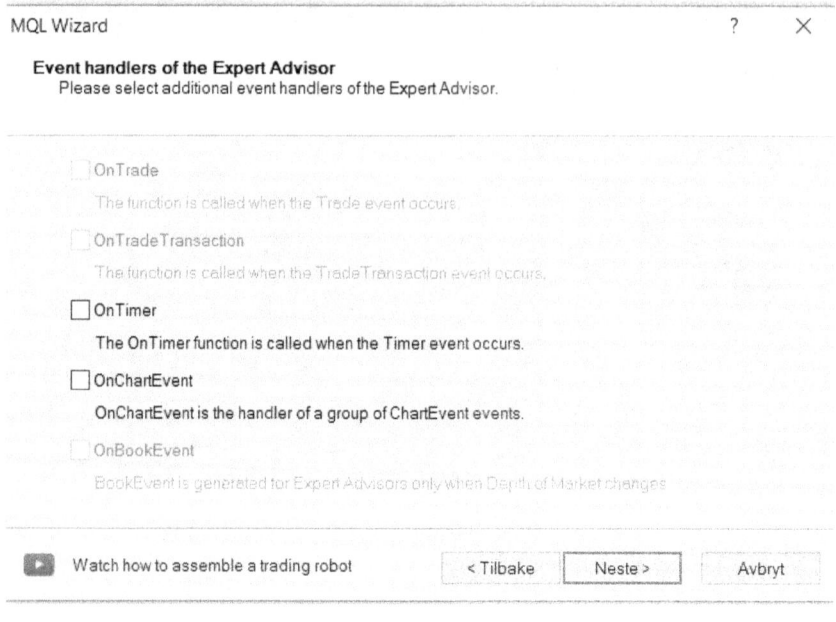

3-6 In the next window tick all the boxes and press next.

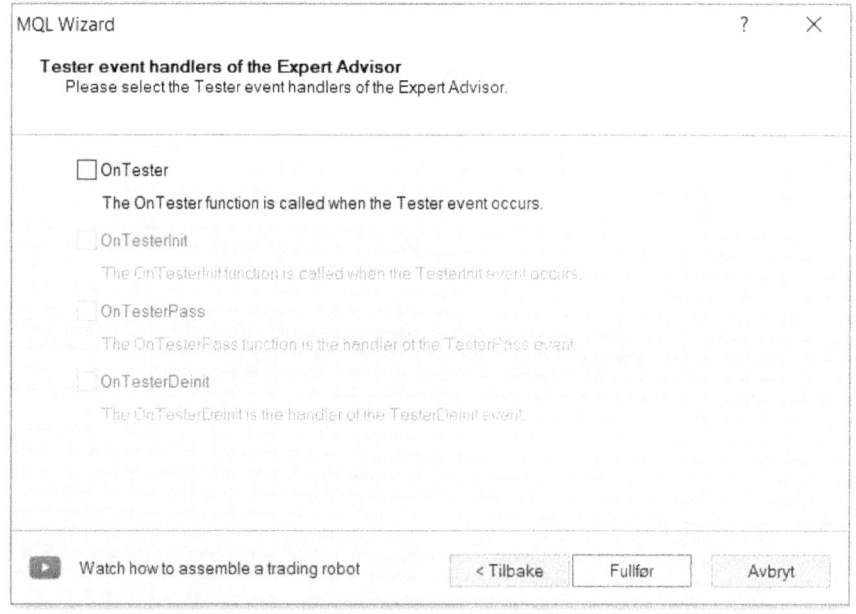

3-7 Also in next window tick all the boxes and press finish(fullfør=finish on English platforms)

3.4 Understanding of script

After finishing the *new expert advisor wizard* we should have created a skull of our first script of our algorithm. We will use this section to explain the illustration 3-8, you can see the script. Begin by examining the script carefully, everything within it, even every dot. Because everything in it has some meaning, and it's sensitive, if you write something wrong you will be unable to run it.

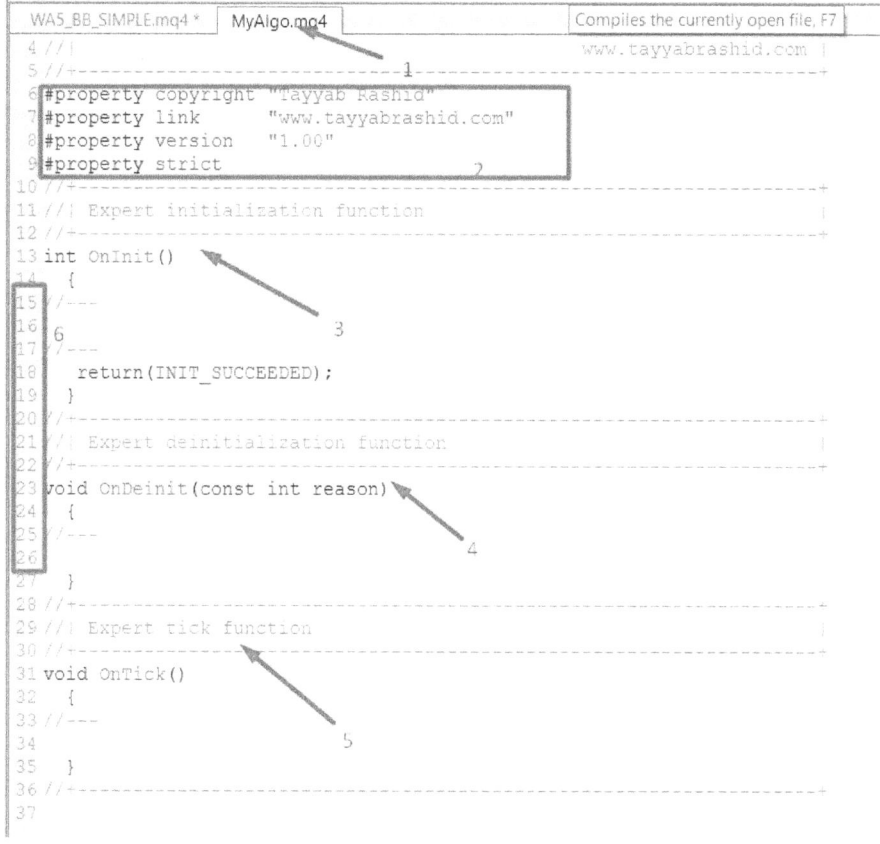

3-8 Empty skull or template of an algorithm(expert advisor).

This whole section is called a script; *this is your algorithm skull.*

11

1. *MyAlgo*, the name you wrote in you wizard. In editor every panel will be an algorithm and each will have its own name.

2. This section, will have everything else you wrote in the wizard, your name, author name and stating that this script is the author's property.

3. A script is built of several functions, and all the functions will be executed when you run your script on a live account or in the strategy tester. You make functions, in the functions you code what you want to do and give inputs. The function takes your input, does the operations you have coded into it and then gives an output that you have told it to give. A function executes all operations in it. As predefined, all scripts comes with three functions, and only these three functions will be used to call on all other functions(functions can call on other functions). You can have the operation in one function that it calls on another function. As you can see on your script you will have three functions. The first is called *int OnInit()* this function will be executed when we begin using this algo, whether we place it on the chart or we use it in the strategy tester. It will be called on only once in the start. This is an expert initialization function.

4. *Void OnDeinit()* this function will be called on at the end, when we detach our algorithm from the chart or stop the strategy tester. This is an expert deinitialization function.

5. The last function to be defined is our tick function. This function is run on every tick, this means every time a trade is executed in the market. So one tick represents one trade.

6. Every line has its own number in the script so it's easy for you to track any errors. It's important to note that when you are writing, the first instruction will be executed first, then the next one and so on.

3.5 Compiler button

Compiler button runs your script and checks for errors, if it has errors it will let you know and you should fix them. Press the compiler button to check for any errors, and check if your algorithm works. Always press compiler button as you code your algorithm to check for errors. If you check for errors at the end it can be difficult to fix so many errors at once. Under the script you will get a new box, if there are no errors it will give an output of 0 errors. It also shows how much time it took to run thru the script, in the box it shows that it took 1407 Milliseconds to run this empty script. If you are trading high frequency it's important to code effectively so that you can decrease the time it takes to run your script.

```
    WA5_BB_SIMPLE.mq4    MyAlgo.mq4
 4 //|
 5 //+-----------------------------------------  www.tayyabrashid.com |
 6 #property copyright "Tayyab Rashid"
 7 #property link      "www.tayyabrashid.com"
 8 #property version   "1.00"
 9 #property strict
10 //+-----------------------------------------------------------------+
11 //| Expert initialization function                                  |
12 //+-----------------------------------------------------------------+
13 int OnInit()
14   {
15 //---
16
17 //---
18    return(INIT_SUCCEEDED);
19   }
20 //+-----------------------------------------------------------------+
21 //| Expert deinitialization function                                |
22 //+-----------------------------------------------------------------+
23 void OnDeinit(const int reason)
24   {
25 //---
26
27   }
28 //+-----------------------------------------------------------------+
29 //| Expert tick function                                            |
30 //+-----------------------------------------------------------------+
31 void OnTick()
32   {
33 //---
34
35   }
36 //+-----------------------------------------------------------------+

 Description
 'MyAlgo.mq4'
 0 error(s), 0 warning(s), compile time: 1407 msec
```

3-9 At the bottom you will get an error messages if something is wrong with your script.

14

4 Introducing Flowcharts

4.1 What is a Flowchart?

When you are coding or programming, you are writing a program which consist of different functions and you make a logic where the different functions are executed one after the other. To understand the logic of a script sometimes it's better to use flowcharts, which we will use in the remainder of the book.

Definition of a Flowchart at Wikipedia:

A flowchart is a type of diagram that represents an algorithm, workflow or process, showing the steps as boxes of various kinds, and their order by connecting them with arrows. This diagrammatic representation illustrates a solution model to a given problem. Flowcharts are used in analyzing, designing, documenting or managing a process or program in various fields.

A script can either run in real-time on a demo or a live account, then you must attach your algorithm to a chart or test in the strategy tester. Under the development of an algorithm you might use the strategy tester frequently and test your algorithm, then run it on your account. In our development, we will only use strategy tester to test our script.

4.2 Objects of a flowchart

Shape	Name	Description
→	Flowline	An arrow coming from one symbol and ending at another symbol represents that control passes to the symbol the arrow points to. The line for the arrow can be solid or dashed. The meaning of the arrow with dashed line may differ from one flowchart to another and can be defined in the legend
⬭	Terminal	Represented as circles, ovals, stadiums or rounded (fillet) rectangles. They usually contain the word "Start" or "End", or another phrase signaling the start or end of a process, such as "submit inquiry" or "receive product".
▭	Process	Represented as rectangles. This shape is used to show that something is performed. Examples: "Add 1 to X", "replace identified part", "save changes", etc...
◇	Decision	Represented as a diamond (rhombus) showing where a decision is necessary, commonly a Yes/No question or True/False test. The conditional symbol is peculiar in that it has two arrows coming out of it, usually from the bottom point and right point, one corresponding to Yes or True, and one corresponding to No or False. (The arrows should always be labeled.)

		More than two arrows can be used, but this is normally a clear indicator that a complex decision is being taken, in which case it may need to be broken-down further or replaced with the "predefined process" symbol. Decision can also help in the filtering of data.
	Input/Output	Represented as a parallelogram. Involves receiving data and displaying processed data. Can only move from input to output and not vice versa. Examples: Get X from the user; display X.
	Predefined	Represented as rectangles with double-struck vertical edges; these are used to show complex processing steps which may be detailed in a separate flowchart. Example: process-files. One subroutine may have multiple distinct entry points or exit flows (see coroutine). If so, these are shown as labeled 'wells' in the rectangle, and control arrows connect to these 'wells'.
	Preparation	Represented as a hexagon. May also be called initialization. Shows operations which have no effect other than preparing a value for a subsequent conditional or decision step. Alternatively, this shape is used to replace the Decision Shape in the case of conditional looping.
	On-page connecter	Generally represented with a circle, showing where multiple control flows converge in a single exit flow. It will have more than one arrow coming into it, but only one going

		out. In simple cases, one may simply have an arrow point to another arrow instead. These are useful to represent an iterative process (what in Computer Science is called a loop). A loop may, for example, consist of a connector where control first enters, processing steps, a conditional with one arrow exiting the loop, and one going back to the connector. For additional clarity, wherever two lines accidentally cross in the drawing, one of them may be drawn with a small semicircle over the other, showing that no connection is intended.

4-1 Explanation of the elements in a flowchart.

4.3 Flowchart of a simple algorithm template

We begin by making a flowchart of the template we created in the last chapter with the predefined functions and see how things work.

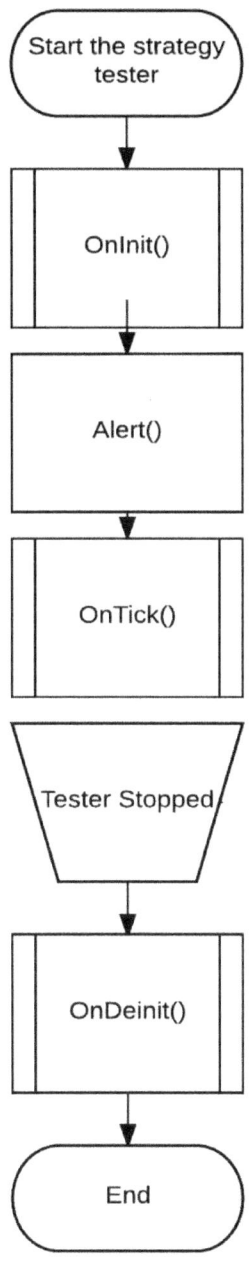

4-2 Flow chart of the simple algorithm template from last chapter.

Explanation of Flow chart in illustration 4-2

1. It starts by you clicking the strategy tester, pressing the button on your platform.

2. Then it executes everything stated in the OnInit() function, it will only execute once.

3. When the initialization function is finished, it is also finished with everything in the OnInit() function. Then it calls the OnTick() function which runs every time a new tick occurs, when a new trade in that instrument has been made. It will continue running this function until the strategy tester is finished(either manually by us or it has run thru all the sample periods).

4. You can stop the strategy tester manually by pressing the *stop* button, or when the run is finished for the time period this will automatically stop it. Please note the shape of the flowchart object, this is the shape of manual operations. So when this event happens it will stop running the script and execute the next operation.

5. When we have stopped the strategy tester, everything in OnDeinit() function will be executed. We have reached the end of the algorithm and our script is finished.

By now you should understand the flow of the predefined functions in our skull. It starts from the top of the flowchart and executes all. After it's finished executing everything in a function, it passes control to the next operation in our flowchart.

Exercise

Try to delete OnDeinit() from the script and then compile. Does it have any impact on the error? Did you get any errors that you have to include in that function?

5 Introducing functions

5.1 What is a function?

Coding is about you designing different functions; you have input into the function and you want it to do something. You can either get an outcome of the function or you could just simply use it to do something like place a trade.

An output function looks like this:

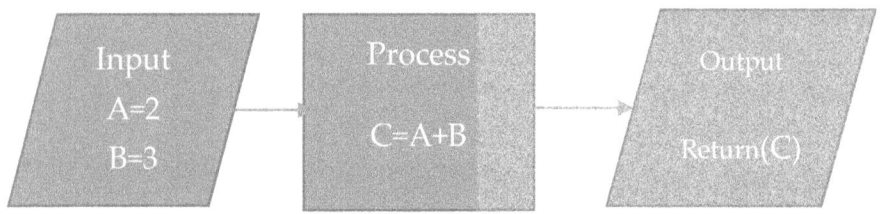

5-1 Illustration of a function that has an output.

You have input variables and assign a value to them. In the process, you add both input values and get a new variable C which holds the added value, which is the output from this function. When you execute this function it will return variable C, which in this case holds a value of 5.

Non-output function look like this:

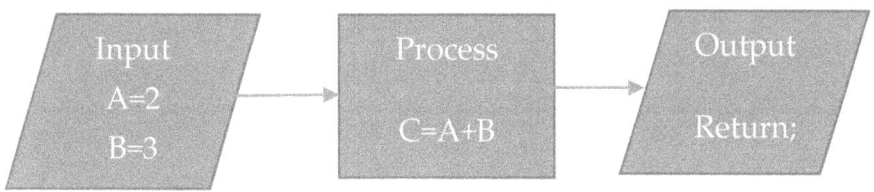

5-1 Illustration of a function which has no output.

This is the other type of function, here you have three variables as inputs A, B and C. They have values assigned to them 2,3 and 0. Also in this we have a process which is adding A+B and assign this added value to variable C. When the process is finished, C will hold the value of 5(A+B = 2+3) and the function will return nothing, and both are called functions. It just gives a new value to our variable C and returns nothing.

5-2 Defining input variables

You can use words and numbers in the function. You must always begin with defining which type of variable it is, name the variable, and then assign the value you want to use in your function.

Let us say you want to make a function that adds 2+3 and we get an answer. If we just write 2+3= this is incorrect, you will get an error message and it will not run.

You begin by defining your input variables. Whole numbers like 2 and 3 are an *integer(int)* type of variable.

You write these input variables like this:

```
int A= ;
int B= ;
int C= ;
```

5-3

All three are integer type of variables, so they begin with the word *int*, a space, and then we write our variable. We want to name that value, our value 2 is named A. So in the process when you want to use the number 2, you use it by writing variable names like C=A+B.

You should also note the semicolon at the end of each variable. Assigning value to each of the variables is a separate operation, and we end each of the operations with a semicolon. Above we have three operations, when the program is reading our script after the semicolon, it knows that one operation is finished. It assigns its value and goes to the next operation, assigning value to the next variable. *We will use a semicolon every time an operation is finished.* It's like a period in a sentence.

5-3 Different types of variables in Mql4

Integer: This variable is whole numbers meaning 1,2,3,4
Example:

```
int ShortMA= ;
int LongMA= ;
```

5-4

We have declared variables which can be input variables for different moving average periods in a moving average function. Note the semicolon again.

Double: This is a variable which is a number with a decimal 1.02, 0.02, etc
Example:

```
double Stoploss=0.0020;
```

5-5

String: Is a text type and must always be written with quotes like "Hedge", "Martigale" or "EURUSD"
Examples:

```
string word="helloword";
```

5-6

Bool: This is a variable which can have value of TRUE or FALSE, it's Boolean type
Example:

```
bool yes=TRUE;
```

5-7

Exercise:

Define which type of variable is:

John, 1.2, 50, 100, and Your Trading System

5.4 types of a function

The types of functions are decided by what outcome you want from them. We can begin by dividing functions in two main groups based on whether they give an output or not.

Output functions type

Integer: Same as input variable, if you are making a function where the output is an integer this is the type of function.

Double: Same as double input variable, if your output is going to have decimals you need this type of function.

String: Same as string input variable, if your output is going to be text type this is your function type.

Boolean: Same as Boolean input variable, if your output is going to either stating false or true its Boolean type.

What they all have in common is that they return something back.

Non-output function type

There is only one type and it's called **void**. This is a function which only executes what is in the function but doesn't give output, it returns nothing. Mostly it's used to calculate another variable we have defined but not assigned a value to as yet, or to execute another function.

5.5 Objects of a function

```
functiontype FunctionName()
{

return;
}
```

5-9

Figure 5-9 shows objects of a function.

Functiontype: Which can be int, double, string or bool if it's output function or void if it's non-output function

FunctionName: Here you will write the name of your function followed by an opening and closing parentheses (). Also look that we have finished a line but this time we are not ending the line with semicolon, this is because we are not finished with this process yet. Like a line alone, this function type and function name doesn't make sense.

Opening and Closing brackets: All the function must be on the line after defining the type and giving the name ending with parentheses. The next line should be opening bracket { that signals the start of the function. Everything you write after the bracket, the following lines will be executed when you call on this function. We close the function with a closing bracket } to define a end of the function, but before the end we have to write *return;* if it's *void* type and *return(what we want to return)* if it's an output function.

Task 1:

Make a function where you have three input variables A, B and C.

A=3

B=4

C=0

Where the function will add A+B and assign the value to C, then C should be the input variable and Name it MyFunction.

```
int MyFunction()
{
    int A= ;
    int B= ;
    int C= ;

    C=A+B;
    return(C);

}
```

Above you can see an output function, since we have an output type integer which is a whole number, the function type is int. Then we give it the name MyFunction(), and set an opening bracket. Then we define all the variables we will use, they are integer type, we end them with semicolons. After giving C the added value, we return C, which means that whenever we call on the function by writing: MyFunction(); equals value 7 which is the return value.

Task 2:

Make a function where you have three input variables A, B and C.

A=3

B=4

C=0

Where the function will add A+B and assign the value to C, then use function Print to Print C and Name it MyFunction.

```
void MyFunction()
{
    int A= ;
    int B= ;
    int C= ;

    C=A+B;
    Print(C);

}
```

We have the same operation in this function but the difference is the type, the aim of the function, it will not return anything. It will just print the value of the C in Terminal Journal. When you call on MyFunction(); now it will return nothing.

5.6 "Hello World" Alerts

Let us play a bit with this so that we get an understanding of how functions work and run our algorithm for the first time. Let us write an operation.

Alert("Hello World");

Alert() is a function in metatrader.

"Hello Word" is the sentence we want displayed, the sentence must be written with quotes. At the end of the operation we indicate that this operation has ended and we close the statement with semicolon ";". Let us see the help file for that function. *You highlight "Alert" and press F1*

Alert

Displays a message in a separate window.

```
void   Alert (
   argument,        // first value
   ...              // other values
   );
```

This function displays message in a separate window.

So we write this function first in OnInit() function and press compile. Like this:

After pressing compile and we get no errors. Then we go to our Metatrader and attempt to run the script.

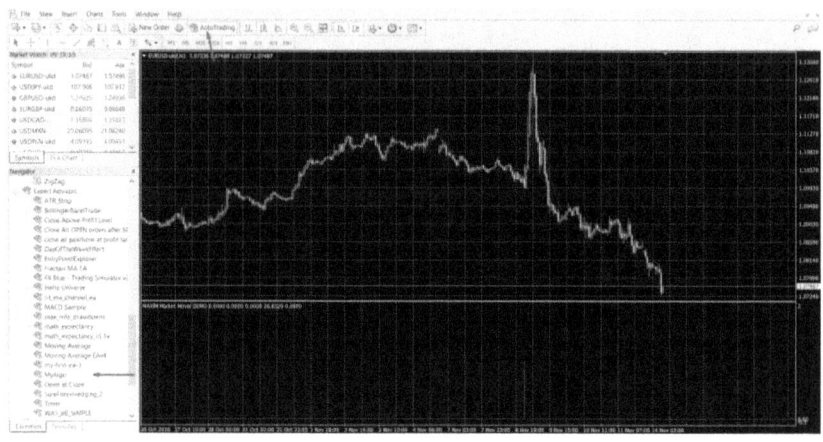

5-12 Go to the terminal enable AutoTrading and drag and drop MyAlgo on your chart.

We must first enable automate trading and then go to our navigator window in the left and drag "MyAlgo" and drop on the chart.

Next window will pop up, just click "OK".

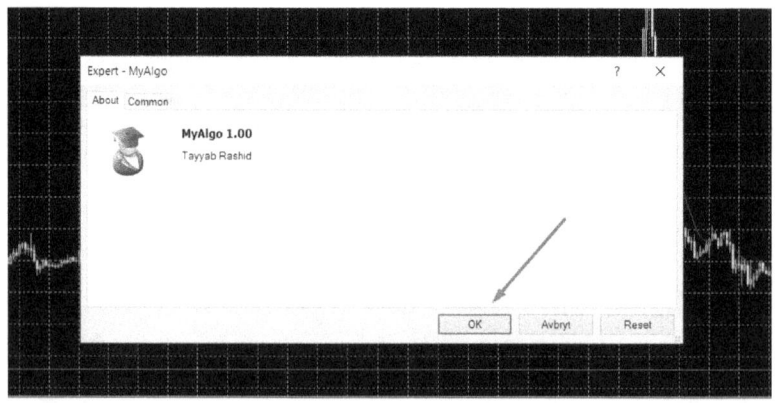

5-12 Just Click on OK.

Now the algorithm is running on this chart and timeframe. Right after you will get Alert, it's because we had the Alert() function in the Initialization(OnInit()) function and this is run once at the start of your algorithm.

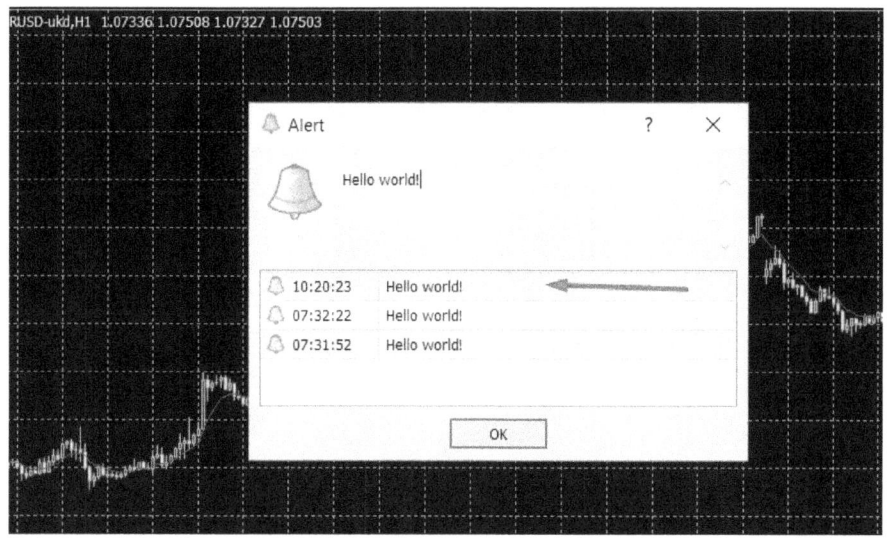

5-13 This is how the Alert will be displayed on your terminal.

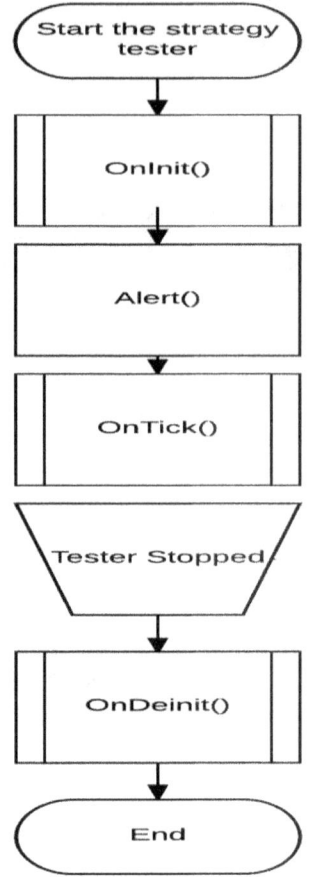

5-14 Flowchart when we have the Alert() function in the OnInit()

You see how the flows progresses, after start, it calls on the OnInit() function which calls on the Alert() function. After executing the Alert() function it then passes control to Ontick() function.

Let us experiment, now put the Alert() function in the Deinitialization function, then compile and drop again on the chart.

First we must remove the Algorithm from the chart. Right click on the chart and open the dropdown menu. Click Expert Advisor - Remove

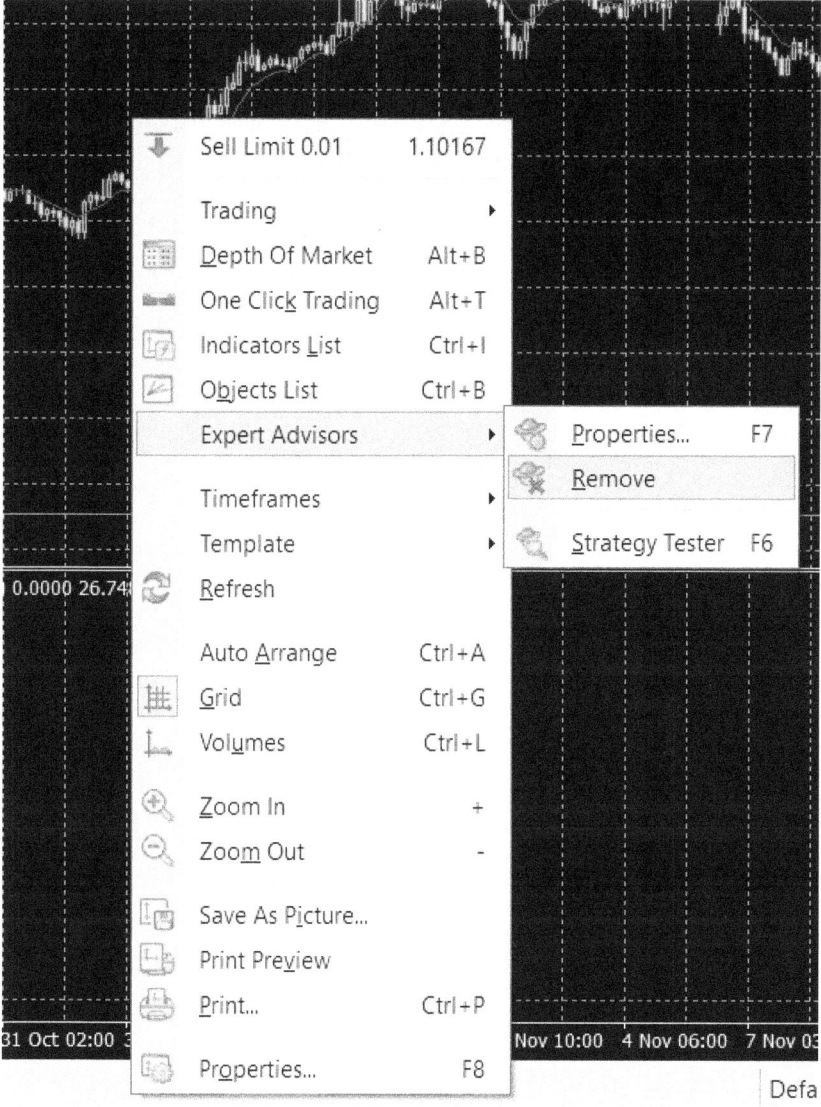

5-15 How you remove your algorithm from the chart or to stop it.

```
WA5_BB_SIMPLE.mq4 | MyAlgo.mq4
 4 //|                                                    www.tayyabrashid.com |
 5 //+---------------------------------------------------------------------+
 6 #property copyright "Tayyab Rashid"
 7 #property link      "www.tayyabrashid.com"
 8 #property version   "1.00"
 9 #property strict
10 //+---------------------------------------------------------------------+
11 //| Expert initialization function                                       |
12 //+---------------------------------------------------------------------+
13 int OnInit()         ◄───────────
14   {
15 //---
16
17 //---
18    return(INIT_SUCCEEDED);
19   }
20 //+---------------------------------------------------------------------+
21 //| Expert deinitialization function                                     |
22 //+---------------------------------------------------------------------+
23 void OnDeinit(const int reason)  ◄───────────
24   {
25 //---
26    Alert("Hello world!");
27   }
28 //+---------------------------------------------------------------------+
29 //| Expert tick function                                                 |
30 //+---------------------------------------------------------------------+
31 void OnTick()
32   {
33 //---
34
35   }
36 //+---------------------------------------------------------------------+
```

5-16 If we put the Alert() function in OnDeinit() functio

Here we have moved our function from OnInit() to OnDeinit().
Again we drag and drop, nothing will happen, but if you now try
to remove your algo from your chart, the Alert will come up.
Because all functions in OnDeinit will run the function when we
stop our algorithm. See diagram 5-17.

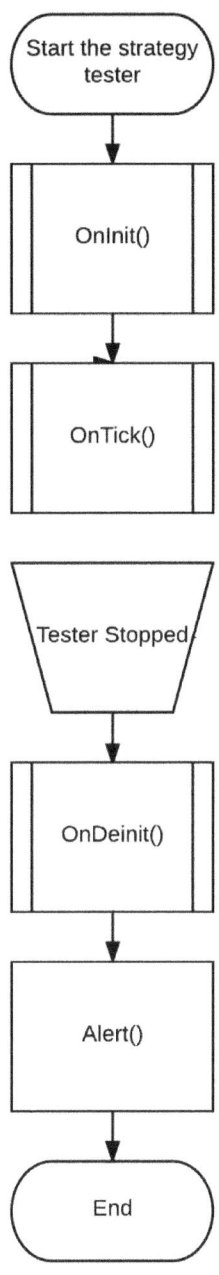

5-17 Flowchart if you put Alert() function in OnDeinit() function.

Let us put our Alert function in the OnTick() function, this runs the function on every tick. You will get messages all the time, until you stop the tester or remove the algorithm from the chart,

```
WA5_BB_SIMPLE.mq4  |  MyAlgo.mq4
 7 #property link        "www.tayyabrashid.com"
 8 #property version     "1.00"
 9 #property strict
10 //+-------------------------------------------------+
11 //|  Expert initialization function
12 //+-------------------------------------------------+
13 int OnInit()
14   {
15 //---
16
17 //---
18    return(INIT_SUCCEEDED);
19   }
20 //+-------------------------------------------------+
21 //|  Expert deinitialization function
22 //+-------------------------------------------------+
23 void OnDeinit(const int reason)
24   {
25 //---
26
27   }
28 //+-------------------------------------------------+
29 //|  Expert tick function
30 //+-------------------------------------------------+
31 void OnTick()
32   {
33 //---
34      Alert("Hello world!");
35   }
36 //+-
```

5-20 This is how we will put the Alert() function in the OnTick() function. We call a function by naming the function with parentheses, an input and ending it with semicolon.

The tick function will call on the Alert() function on every tick, every time a new trade has happened.

After compiling your algorithm, you drag your algo from the navigator windows and drop it on the chart again. You will now see that the Alert function is called frequently on every tick on your screen.

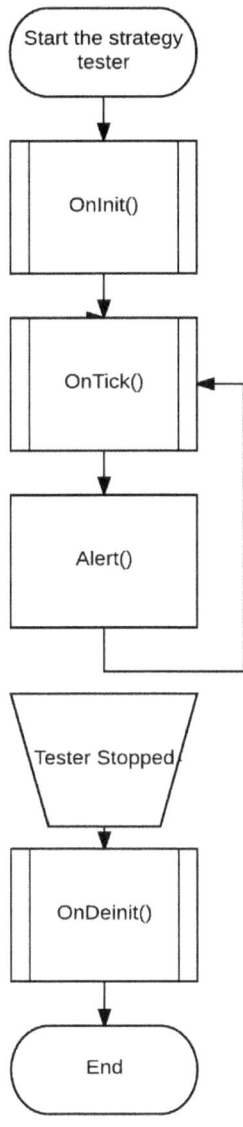

5-19 Flowchart when you put Alert() function in the OnTick() function.

What you should know now.

- How to begin writing a script – New Algo
- OnInit(), OnDeinit() and Ontick() functions
- How to compile your algo
- How to run your Algo
- How to stop your running Algo
- How to display an Alert

5.7 Declare different input variables

There are two places. One of the places is called global area, the variables declared here can be used in any of the other functions, and this area is above all the functions, above the OnInit() function also.

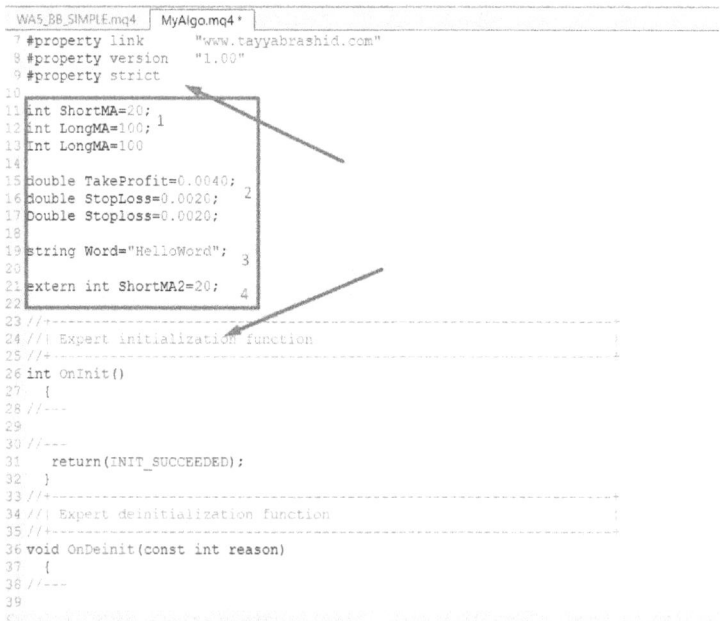

5-20 How we declare input variables in the global area.

40

1. To declare an integer variable we use *int,* it's important to note that this programming language is case sensitive so if you write *INT or Int* you will get an error message. You see that when we write int the correct way we get that word in blue but when we write Int we get that word in black, which is incorrect. Next, which is important, you see in line 13 that we don't have a semicolon after the statement, this mean we haven't closed this statement, then it's another error.

   So four takeaways from this:
   1. int= this is an integer type of variable
   2. Name of the variable is *ShortMA*
   3. The value assigned to this variable is 20
   4. We close every stand alone statement with a semicolon;

2. We use *double* to tell which type of variable this is, this is a variable with a numeric value that includes decimals, and we assign a value to it.

3. We use *string* to tell which type of variable this is, name of the variable is a *word* and then we assign "HelloWorld" as value, *remember* the quotes and we add and close this operation or statement with a semicolon.

4. All these variables are declared above all other functions, this is key because then we can use them in all the functions below. This program executes the first statement

first and then below. So, if you have a function on line 5 but the variable used in the function is on line 15, then this function will not have a variable to use because it's not declared. *All these variables are declared outside of any function, this means all of them can be used in any functions below, but if we declared a variable within a function we can only use that variable in that particular function.*

Last in the picture above you can see that the last variable has *extern* written in front of it. This is because now we can change this variable when we are testing the strategy(running this algorithm) and we can optimize it.

In the script above if you delete lines 13 and 17 and then compile you will get no errors and you can run your script. Then drag and drop this algo on any chart and you will get a box, click on the panel called *input,* you will see that only the variable where we have *extern* before it can be changed. Therefore, if you use a variable that you want to be changeable you simply need to write *extern* before it.

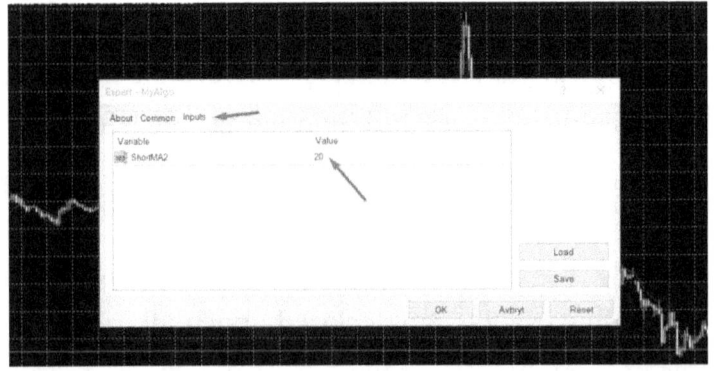

5-21 Input box when you use extern variables.

42

Picture 5-21 illustrates how we use local variables, those variables are declared within the function and can only be used by this function.

```
void MyFunction()
{
    int A= ;
    int B= ;
    int C= ;

    C=A+B;
    Print(C);

}
```

5-21 This shows how the input variables appear in the local area.

We use *global variable* when we want to change the input variable later when we are running the strategy or optimizing it. It can be used in the global area when there are several functions using the same input variable. Maybe you have designed a function where you assign value to a variable using function one, and then a variable with an assigned value by function one is used by function two.

What you should know from this session:
- Different types of variables used, string, integer and double
- How to declare a variable
- How to end a statement or operation
- That this programming language is case sensitive must write right letter
- Where in the script variables should be declared
- How to declare changeable variables

6 NewOrder() Function

6.1 Description of the function

We are going to make a function called NewOrder() this will be a void type of function, and returns nothing. Remember for *void* we have to write it in lower case.

6.2 Creating the function

```
void NewOrder()
{
return;
}
```

6-1 We start by writing void, Name of the function, opening and closing bracket.

This is the start of writing the function, we have not written anything in it yet, it's an empty skull. It is opening and closing of the function. The *type is void because this function will not return anything,* name is NewOrder followed by opening and closing parentheses. On next line we have an opening bracket and then write *return;* before the closing bracket of the function.

```
WA5_BB_SIMPLE.mq4    MyAlgo.mq4 *
12 //| Expert initialization function
13 //+---------------------------------------------------------+
14 int OnInit()
15   {
16 //---
17
18 //---
19    return(INIT_SUCCEEDED);
20   }
21 //+---------------------------------------------------------+
22 //| Expert deinitialization function
23 //+---------------------------------------------------------+
24 void OnDeinit(const int reason)
25   {
26 //---
27
28   }
29 //+---------------------------------------------------------+
30 //| Expert tick function
31 //+---------------------------------------------------------+
32 void OnTick()
33   {
34 //---
35
36   }
37 //+---------------------------------------------------------+
38 //+---------------------------------------------------------+
39 //|Our own New order send function
40 //+---------------------------------------------------------+
41 void NewOrder()
42 {
43 return;
44 }|
```

6-3 The new function is below all the other functions, the predefined functions.

It's important to know that all the functions we build will be written below our predefined functions in the script.

We will now make a function which has the following input variables in the global area:

extern double TakeProfit=0.0050

extern double StopLoss=0.0025

extern double LotSize=0.01

All of them have extern which means they can be changed when we are running this strategy or in the strategy tester.

OrderSend()

This is an integer type of function. Which returns a value of 1 if the market order has opened and a negative value if the market order was not opened successfully.

int Result=OrderSend(); *We have a storing variable called Result which will store the value this function is returning.*

OrderSend() function has some input variables, which you separated by comma.

1. Symbol, this one we will write as Symbol() because this function will return the symbol of the chart this algorithm is running on

2. Order type we have 6 different order types
   a. OP_BUY=Market buy order
   b. OP_SELL=Market Sell order
   c. OP_BUYLIMIT=Buy limit order
   d. OP_BUYSTOP =Buy stop order
   e. OP_SELLLIMIT=Sell limit order
   f. OP_SELLSTOP=Sell stop order

3. Amount or lotsize since we can either write lotsize directly here or have a variable which we have assigned a lotsize amount to and write it instead.

4. Price can be either ask or bid. Since we want to buy we use the current ask price. We will never get our order filled at bid price if we want to buy. Just try to use bid and you will not get any trades filled if buying.

5. Slippage, how much slippage do we allow, meaning what can be the difference between the price we see as bid and the actual price we get for our order. We will set it to 3 pips.

6. Stoploss, if we set it as 0, we will not have any stop loss. We can either write a value right into this field our assign value to a variable and write the variable instead. We have already assigned a value to our variable StopLoss so we will use that instead. Because this a buy order we have to subtract stoploss from the ask price, and that price level will be our stop loss.

7. Same as Stoploss, we will use a Takeprofit variable. But with buy orders we must add takeprofit to the ask price, to get our take profit level.

8. Comment, if we want any comment to be displayed we write it as a string with quotes or NULL if we don't want any comment. We have used NULL here.

9. Magicnumber: We use 1234. This is not anything special but you might have a different magicnumber if you are running several algorithms on the same pair.

10. This variable is expiration time, when you want this order to be cancelled, if you set it to 0, it will never be cancelled. This variable is in seconds.

11. Arrow, if you want to mark any arrow on the chart when this trade executes you write it here, but we don't want it so we write just clrNONE.

By now you should have finished your OrderSend() function and closed with a closing parentheses and semicolon, you should have this function:

```
void NewOrder()
{
    int
Result=OrderSend(Symbol(),OP_BUY,LotSize,Bid, ,StopLoss,TakeProfit,NULL,    , ,clrNONE);
return;
}
```

6-4 Our first NewOrder() function is finished.

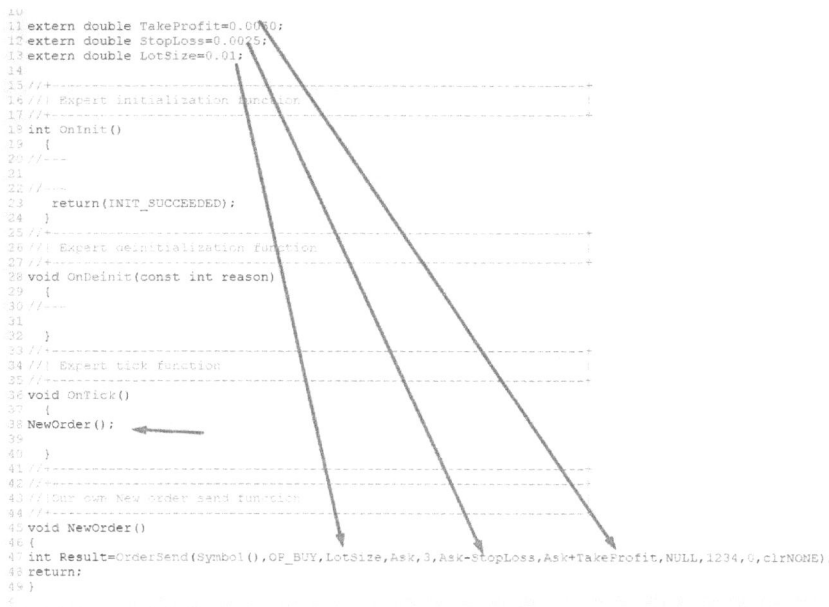

```
10
11 extern double TakeProfit=0.0060;
12 extern double StopLoss=0.0025;
13 extern double LotSize=0.01;
14
15 //+------------------------------------------------------------------+
16 //| Expert initialization function                                   |
17 //+------------------------------------------------------------------+
18 int OnInit()
19   {
20 //---
21
22 //---
23    return(INIT_SUCCEEDED);
24   }
25 //+------------------------------------------------------------------+
26 //| Expert deinitialization function                                 |
27 //+------------------------------------------------------------------+
28 void OnDeinit(const int reason)
29   {
30 //---
31
32   }
33 //+------------------------------------------------------------------+
34 //| Expert tick function                                             |
35 //+------------------------------------------------------------------+
36 void OnTick()
37   {
38 NewOrder();
39
40   }
41 //+------------------------------------------------------------------+
42 //+------------------------------------------------------------------+
43 //| Our own New order send function                                  |
44 //+------------------------------------------------------------------+
45 void NewOrder()
46 {
47 int Result=OrderSend(Symbol(),OP_BUY,LotSize,Ask,3,Ask-StopLoss,Ask+TakeProfit,NULL,1234,0,clrNONE);
48 return;
49 }
```

6-5 External input variables are in the global area before all the functions even predefined ones.

You see that all variables are declared in the beginning, the function is below all three predefined functions.

The variables are defined above all the functions and they are used in the function. We use the name of the variables rather than the values themselves in our function. The OrderSend() function ends with semicolon because this operation is finished, then as we close the whole function with return;. You can see that we call on the function NewOrder(), which calls on OrderSend() with all of our input parameters.

Now you just have to call on this function NewOrder(), this is done by writing NewOrder() in our tick function. Because every time a new tick comes in, all things stated in tick function will be run. Let us place this new function here, remember these functions also need to end with semicolon to close this operation. See line 38. You call a function by writing the name of the function with opening and closing parentheses followed by a semicolon. As shown in the picture below:

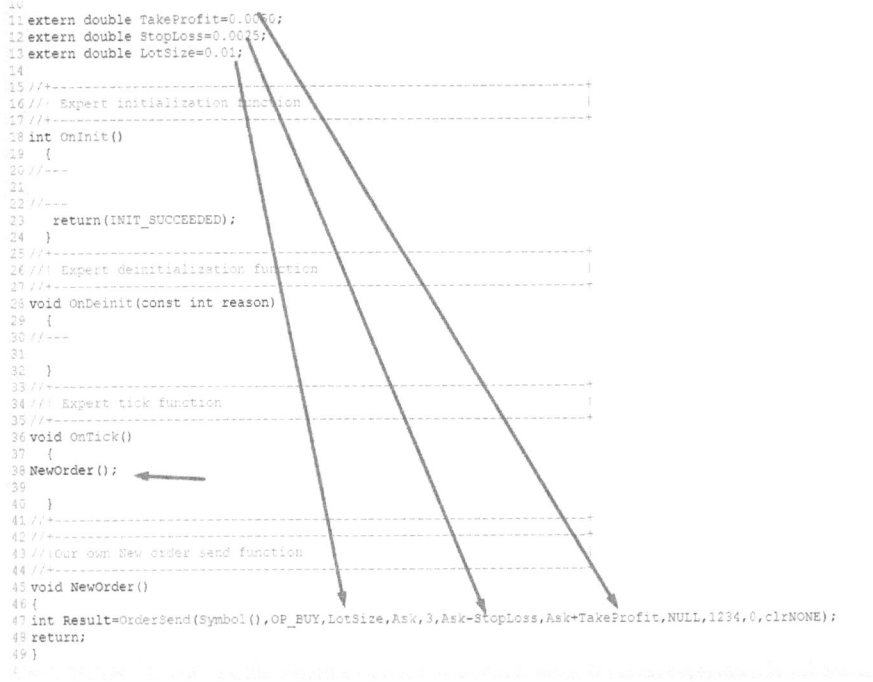

```
11 extern double TakeProfit=0.0056;
12 extern double StopLoss=0.0025;
13 extern double LotSize=0.01;
14
15 //+--------------------------------------------------+
16 //| Expert initialization function                   |
17 //+--------------------------------------------------+
18 int OnInit()
19   {
20 //---
21
22 //---
23    return(INIT_SUCCEEDED);
24   }
25 //+--------------------------------------------------+
26 //| Expert deinitialization function                 |
27 //+--------------------------------------------------+
28 void OnDeinit(const int reason)
29   {
30 //---
31
32   }
33 //+--------------------------------------------------+
34 //| Expert tick function                             |
35 //+--------------------------------------------------+
36 void OnTick()
37   {
38 NewOrder();
39
40   }
41 //+--------------------------------------------------+
42 //+--------------------------------------------------+
43 //|Our own New order send function
44 //+--------------------------------------------------+
45 void NewOrder()
46 {
47 int Result=OrderSend(Symbol(),OP_BUY,LotSize,Ask,3,Ask-StopLoss,Ask+TakeProfit,NULL,1234,0,clrNONE);
48 return;
49 }
```

6-6 How our Neworder() function is used in the tick function

Now you can compile this file.

Press F4 – to open the platform

Press Ctrl+R – to open the strategytester

Now choose MyAlgo file, run on EURUSD, on Tickdata and the timeframe you want.

Because you are running the NewOrder() function in the Tick() function it will place a new order on every tick, so it's going to be many orders. You can see in the flowchart below that after it has placed an order it gives again control to the OnTick() function which calls on the NewOrder() function until the tester has stopped. Congrats! You have now run your first script.

What you should know:

- How to build a function
- How to run on strategy tester

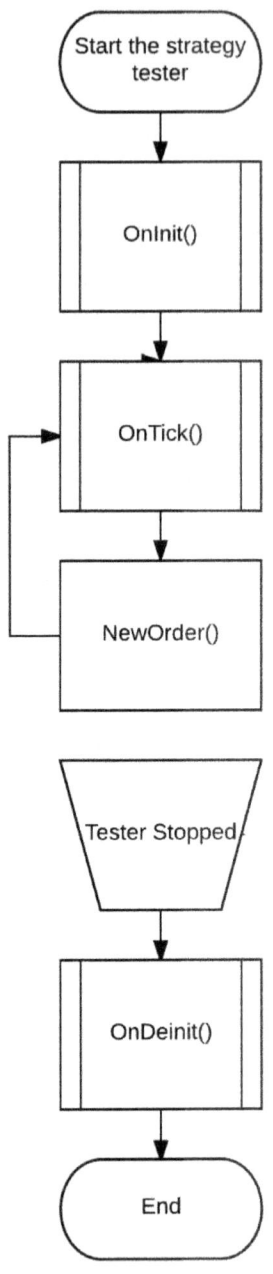

6-7 Flowchart with NewOrder() function.

7 IsNewBar function

The problem with the previous function is that it sends new orders on every tick, so let us make a function which checks whether a new tick also represents new bar or this tick belongs to the same bar as the previous. We need to check this because we only want to run our strategy once on each bar.

7.1 Function description

We will design a Boolean function that will return true if there is a new candle on the chart and return false if there isn't a new candle. It will check this on every tick used in the tick function before the NewOrder() function.

Function description: This function will be checked on every tick and on every tick this function will return TRUE if it's a new candle and FALSE if it's the same candle.

Function name: IsNewCandle()

```
bool IsNewCandle()
{
    static int BarsOnChart=0;
    if(Bars==BarsOnChart)
    return(false);
    BarsOnChart = Bars;
    return(true);
}
```

7-1 This is the full function IsNewCandle().

We will make a flowchart which explains this function.

1. We begin by writing type which is a bool(because it will return false/true) and the name of the function which is IsNewCandle(), then an opening and closing bracket.

2. We declare a variable static int BarOnChart=0; which stores the number of bars on the chart. This variable will be static, meaning that when this function is executed on every tick it will store the number of bars. This is to ensure that the next time we run this function we will compare the number of bars on the chart with the last time we executed it.

3. We use an if-statement which is a decision-making statement. We ask if the bars on the chart on this particular tick are the same as the last time, we store the number of bars. As mentioned, we do this by using an if-statement and equal sign (==). By using function *Bars* this returns the numbers of bars since we started running this algorithm.

4. Independent of whether it's true or false, we assign the number of bars to our BarsOnChart variable.

5. If the bars on the chart has changed, the if-statement is answered with no, we return true;

6. If the bars on chart have not changed, the if-statement is answered with no, this function returns false.

Until we get a tick which is part of a new candle this function will return false. If you are running a one hour timeframe and this candle is a part of new hour it will return true.

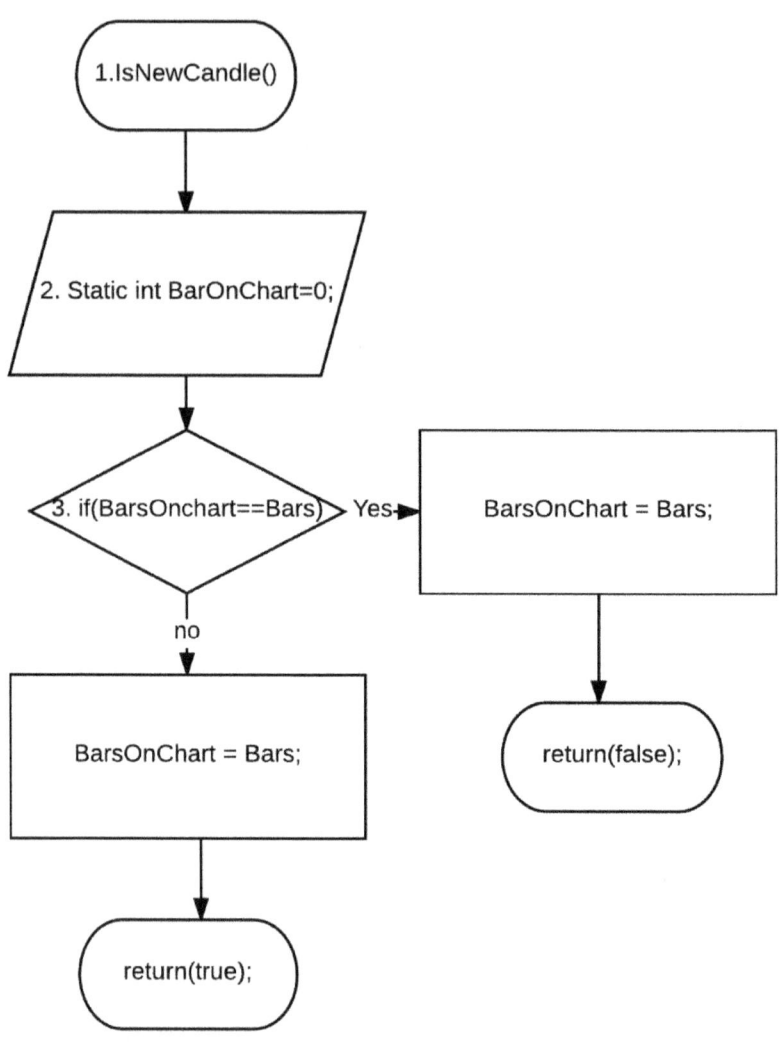

7-2 flow chart of IsNewCandle() function.

```
//+--------------------------------------------------------------+
//|Our own New order send function                               |
//+--------------------------------------------------------------+
void NewOrder()
{
int Result=OrderSend(Symbol(),OP_BUY,LotSize,Ask,3,Ask-StopLoss,Ask+TakeProfit,NULL,1234,0,clrNONE);
return;
}

bool IsNewCandle()
{
    static int BarsOnChart=0;
    if(Bars==BarsOnChart)
    return(false);
    BarsOnChart = Bars;
    return(true);
}
```

7-3 Here you can see our latest function under our previous function in the script.

7.2 How to use IsNewCandle() function

The aim of this new candle function is to only trade once per candle, this means we will put our NewOrder() function within the brackets of the if(IsNewCandle) statement

7-4 You can see how we change the flow of the Ontick function, we rearranged it.

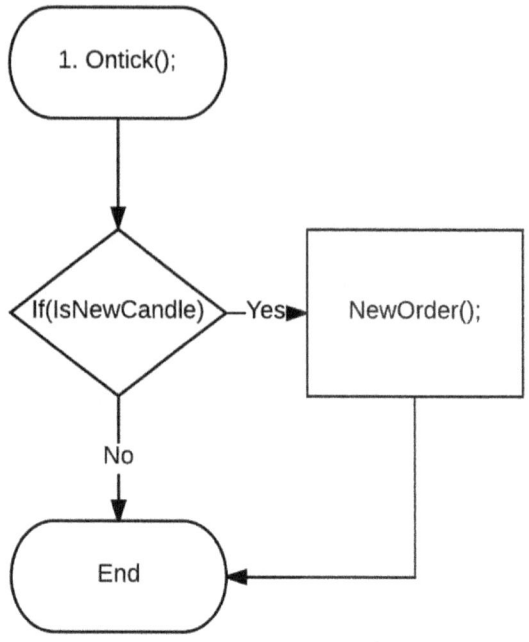

7-4 Rearranged ontick function with IsNewCandle().

You can see that we have changed the OnTick() function. We have added an if-statement which runs the NewOrder() function only if there is a new candle.

You can see that when the Ontick() function executes, it executes if-statement which runs the function IsNewCandle(), if is NewCandle() returns true, it means yes it will execute the NewOrder() function, but if IsNewCandle() returns false it will just go to the end of the new function, and run the same way on the next tick.

What you should know:
-   How to make a bool function
-   What bars functions means
-   If statement, how we use this

8 Total orders function

8.1 Function description

This function counts the number of market orders we have in the market. The goal is to know how many open orders we have to prevent opening more than one market order at a time.

Function name: TotalOpenTrader()

```
int TotalOpenOrders()
{
int Trades= ;
int Total=OrdersTotal();
    for(int i=Total;i>0;i--)
        {
        bool res=OrderSelect(i- ,SELECT_BY_POS,MODE_TRADES);
        if(OrderType()==OP_BUY || OrderType()==OP_SELL)
            {
            Trades++;
            }
        }
    return(Trades);
}
```

8-1 This is how the function looks.

Since this will return a whole number which is the number of orders this is an integer type of function.

1. We start by declaring a variable int Trades and assign a value of zero, this is the variable we will assign the number of open trades to.

2. We begin another function which is also integer type, we assign value of OrdersTotal() to *Total*, this function returns the total open and pending orders in our open trade pool.

3. We create a for loop. This is a loop which will iterate the number of all pending orders and open orders if the number is above zero, and it will decrease the value of i after each loop, as long as i is greater than or equal to zero.

4. Next it will check if the value of i is above zero, if there are any orders in the terminal it will be above zero, like 2.

5. If we don't have any orders in the terminal it will just execute Return(Trades); which will return 0, and pass the control outside of this function.

6. If i is above zero it will run thru the rest of the loop.

7. First process is to select the particular order in our trade pool. We do this by using our OrderSelect() function, this function will return true if there is a trade in our open trade or else false. If the statement with OrderSelect() combined has two operations in our function, one is to select the right order and since it is a boolean type return of the function, it will return true which then passes

control to the next operation. OrderSelect has three variables, first variable is index of the trade we are running thru the loop, we must set i-1, because the first trade has an index value of zero. The next variable we use indicates that we select the trade by its position in the index. Then we tell it that we want to use the live trade pool, not to select historical trades. OrderSelect() is a Boolean type of variable which returns true if we have any trades selected and false if no trades are selected.

8. Then we have an if-statement, which checks whether the trade we have selected is a buy or sell market order.

9. If it's a buy or sell order we add 1 to our variable Trades, if not it will just pass control back to for loop to decrease i. If we have 8 total orders in the pool, next time i will have the value of 7 in the loop.

10. When it has run thru all open orders i will have a value of 0, and then the control will be passed to return(Trades) which return Trades variable to whom may be calling on this function. So if there are 7 market orders, variable Trades will have a value of 7 when we return(Trades) outside the function.

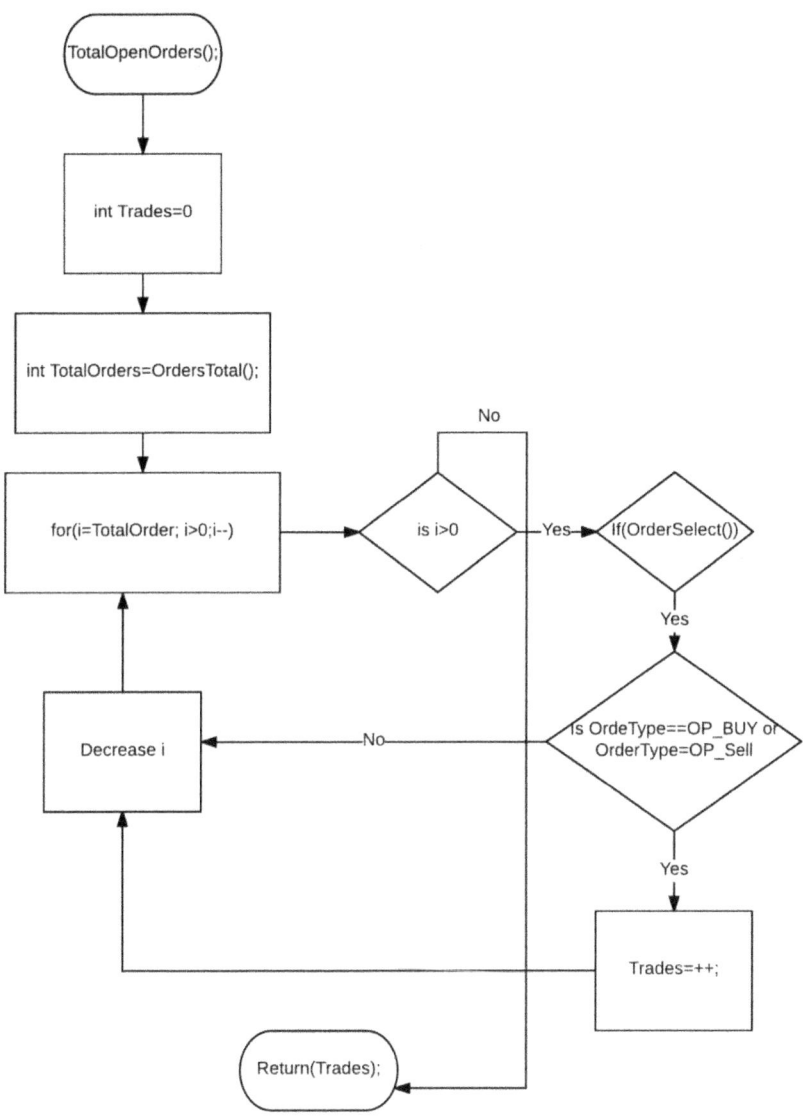

8-2 Flow chart for the TotalOpenOrders().

8.2 How to use TotalOpenOrder() function

We will now use our new function in our tick function to check and only trade if there are no open orders, meaning if TotalOpenOrder()<1.

```
25 //+--------------------------------------------------------------+
26 //| Expert deinitialization function                              |
27 //+--------------------------------------------------------------+
28 void OnDeinit(const int reason)
29   {
30 //---
31
32   }
33 //+--------------------------------------------------------------+
34 //| Expert tick function                                          |
35 //+--------------------------------------------------------------+
36 void OnTick()
37   {
38   if(IsNewCandle())
39     {
40       if(TotalOpenOrders()<1)
41         {
42           NewOrder();
43         }
44     }
45   }
46 //+--------------------------------------------------------------+
47 //+--------------------------------------------------------------+
48 //!Our own New order send function                                |
49 //+--------------------------------------------------------------+
50 void NewOrder()
51 {
52 int Result=OrderSend(Symbol(),OP_BUY,LotSize,Ask,3,Ask-StopLoss,Ask+TakeProfit,NULL,1234,0,clrNONE);
53 return;
54 }
```

8-3 This is our rearranged OnTick() function.

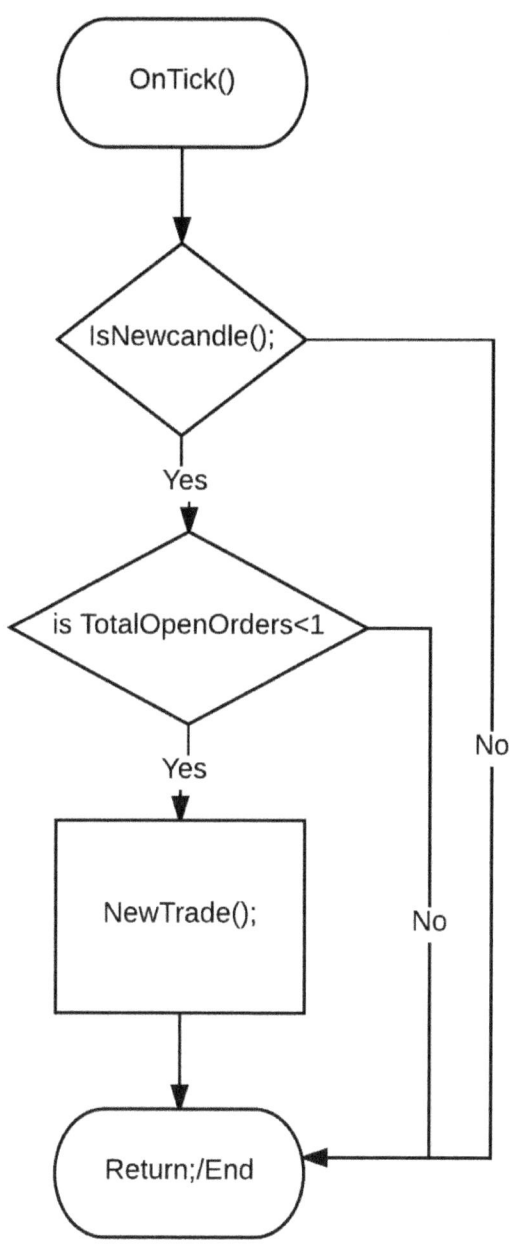

8-4 Flowchart of the rearranged Tick function.

This is how the flow runs, if it's NewCandle it will pass the control to check if total open orders is less than one meaning zero, if that's the case it will pass control to NewTrade() and execute that function NewTrade() function.

You see that we have introduced a new if-statement in our OnTick() function and now we have an additional open and closing bracket. Therefore NewTrade() is within the brackets of TotalOpenTraders statements which is within the IsNewCandle opening and closing brackets. You see the relationship in the flowchart.

9 Close all orders function

9.1 Function description:

We will make a function that closes all market orders and delete all current pending orders.

Function name: CloseAllOrder()

```
void CloseAllOrders()//1.
{
int Total=OrdersTotal(); //2.
    for(int i=Total;i> ;i--) //3.
        {
        if(OrderSelect(i- ,SELECT_BY_POS,MODE_TRADES))//4.
            {
            if(OrderType()==OP_SELL)//5.
                {
                bool res1=OrderClose(OrderTicket(),OrderLots(),Ask, ,clrNONE);//6.
                }
            if(OrderType()==OP_BUY)//7.
                {
                bool res2= OrderClose(OrderTicket(),OrderLots(),Bid, ,clrNONE);//8.
                }
            if(OrderType()==OP_BUYLIMIT || OrderType()==OP_BUYSTOP|| OrderType()==OP_SELL-
STOP||OrderType()==OP_SELLLIMIT)//9.
                {
                bool res3= OrderDelete(OrderTicket(),clrNONE);//10.
                }
            }
        }
return;
}
```

9-1 This is the CloseAllOrder function.

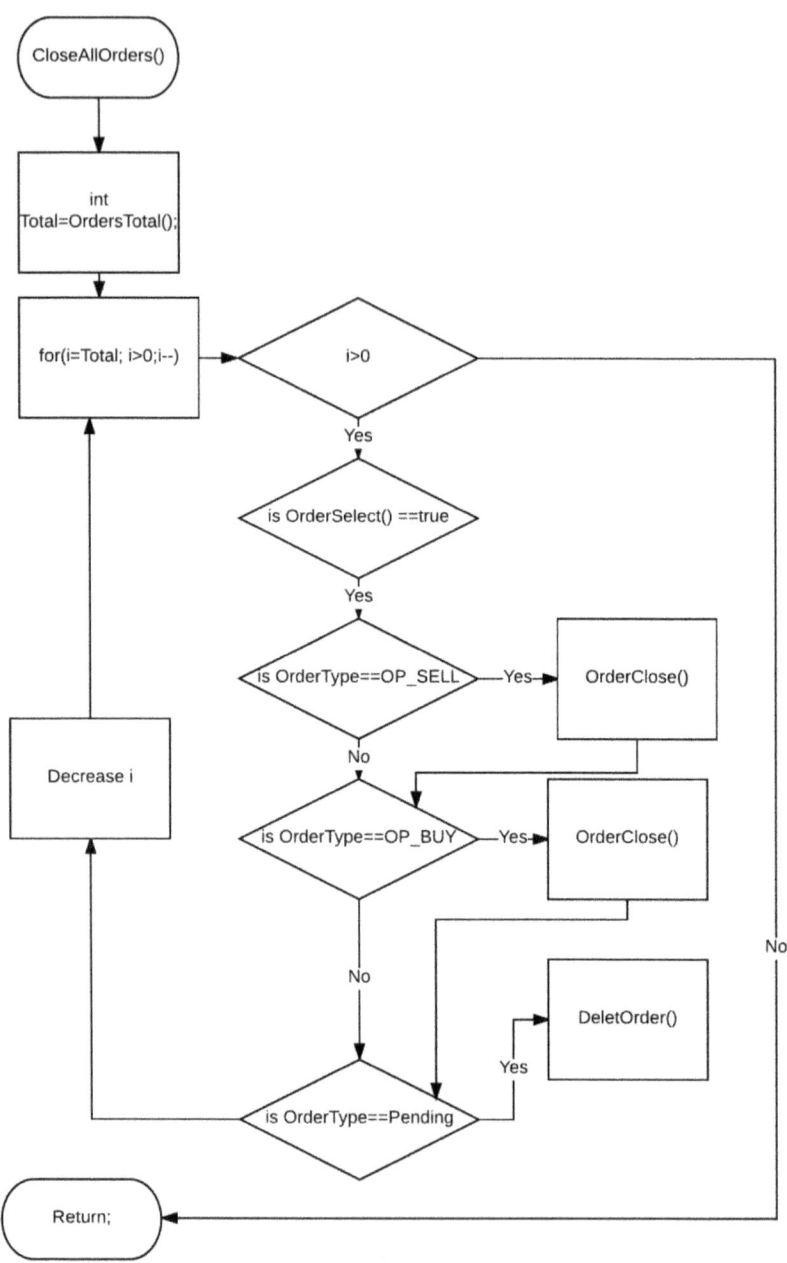

9-2 Flowchart for CloseAllOrder() function.

See the numbers marked in the function and read the comments.

1. We start by writing void + function name + adding open and close brackets and writing return;. Before the closing bracket we will include the rest of the function between the brackets and before the return; statement.

2. Create integer variable name Total, OrdersTotal() function will return the number of total current market and pending orders.

3. Create a for loop which will loop all the orders thru the loop, beginning with the last order. It will need its own opening and closing brackets, everything we want to loop must be within these brackets. If it is a total of 8 orders, it will start by the last number, 8, and run this particular order thru everything we have in our loop. After it is finished it will take order number 7 and continue until order number 1.

4. We use our OrderSelect() function to select the particular order in our order pool, for ex. we have 8 orders, order number 8 will have index number 7 in the pool. It will return true if an order is selected, if there is no order in order pool it will not run this loop, so this if-statement will always be true.

5. This will check if the selected ordertype is a market order and is a sell order, by using OrderType() function which

will return ordertype. If that's the case is it will execute the next operation, which is CloseOrder().

6. We have a semicolon, because this is the end of this loop, OrderClose returns a TRUE/FALSE statement so we use bool res1 to store this value, same with the OrderDelete() function, it will also return true. This function has three input variables.

7.
   a. First variable is OrderTicket() of the selected order
   b. Second variable is the amount you want to close, meaning OrderLots()
   c. Third is the price, since the selected order is sell order we use Ask as the closing price
   d. Fourth variable is slippage we set it to three pips
   e. Comment
8. This will check if the selected order is a market order, if it is a buy order it will execute the next operation.

9. We have semicolon, because this is the end of this loop, we close with the bid price because this is a buy order.

10. This will check whether the selected order is pending or not.

11. We use OrderDelete() to delete this particular order if it's a limit order.

9.2 Use of CloseAllOrder() function

This function will be used by another function which is CandleClose() function which we will create later in the book.

10 Pips function

10.1 Description of the function

Some brokers are four digits others are five digits. This means some are denoting prices in 1.5000, other brokers are denoting prices in 1.50000. You need a function that retrieves 0.0001 if it's four digits and 0.00001 if it's a five. I need a variable double pip, which I want to assign 0.0001 value to. The point is to have a variable that you can multiply with an integer variable to convert that to pips, for example, use it in deciding the stop loss and take profit.

You have an external integer variable called extern int Stoploss=50;

It's a integer variable stating that the stoploss should be 50 pips. When you are applying this variable you want it to be 0.0050 which is 50 pips. You can do this by having a variable called pips that you assign a value of 0.0001 to it. You can then multiply Stoploss*pips=50*0.0001=0.0050 and get the value you want to use in your function.

This function should only run once in the beginning when we start our algorithm in our OnInit() function and assign a new value to our *double pips* variable in the global area.

```
void PipsFunction()//1.
{
double ticksize=MarketInfo(Symbol(),MODE_TICKSIZE);//2.
    if (ticksize == 0.00001 || ticksize == 0.001)//3.
    {
    pips = ticksize*10;//4.
    }
    else
    {
    pips = ticksize;//5.
    }
return;
}
```

10-1 This is the PipFunction.

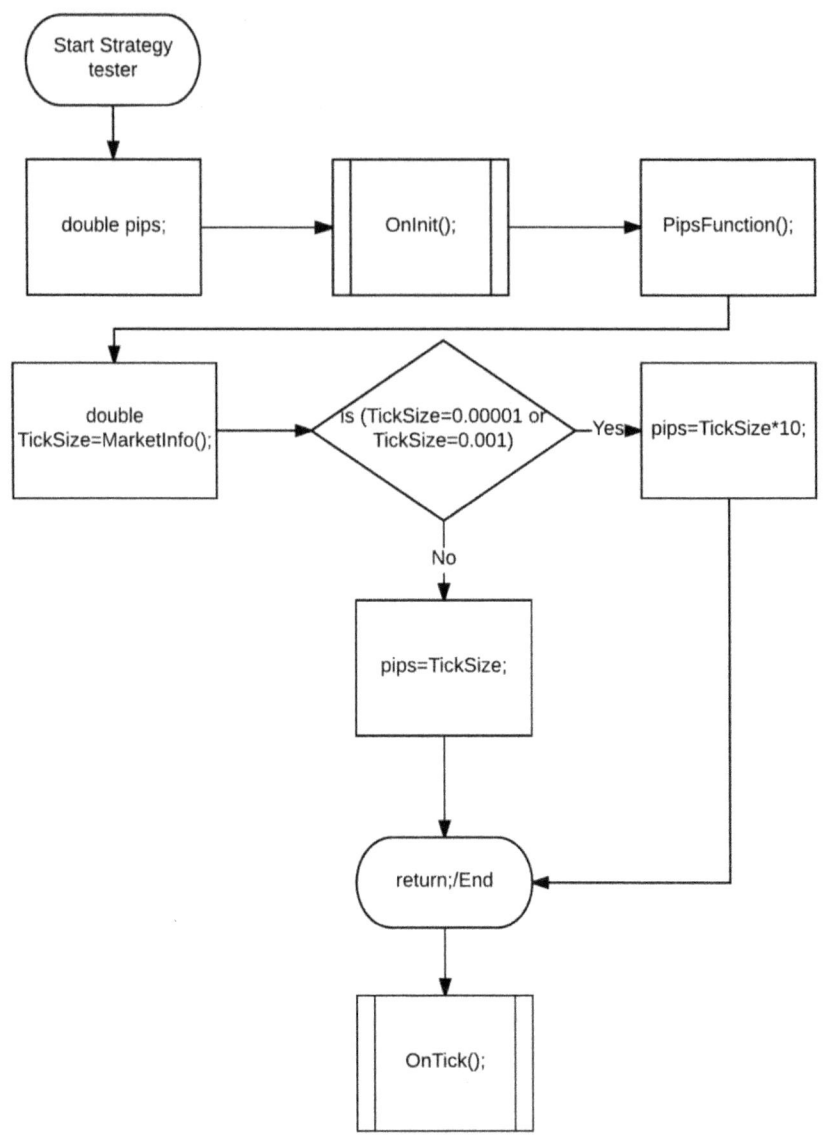

10-2 Flowchart for PipsFunction;

Comment to the function:

You see that first we begin the strategy tester, which then defines the variable double pips, and it gets no value because we will use PipsFunction() to assign value to it. Then control passes to the OnInit() function which calls on the PipsFunction();

1. We start by defining the function, it's a void function with the name PipsFunction() and we add an opening and closing brackets with return; before the closing bracket in the end. This is a function that only executes and returns nothing.

2. We have a double variable TickSize, which equals MarketInfo(Symbol(),MODE_TICKSIZE); we close this operation with a semicolon. MarketInfo() function, retrieves information from the market, which if it's a five digit broker it will retrieve 0.00001 and if it's four digit broker it will retrieve 0.0001 for example on EURUSD pair.

3. Then we have an if-statement which checks whether or not the broker is five digits. If in the last operation it retrieved a value of 0.00001 (TickSize), this is a five digit broker. Then we multiply TickSize with 10 and assign the value to our variable pips: If the TickSize is 0.0001 this means it's a four digits broker then we just use the same value to pips, and there is no need for multiplying it because it already holds the value 0.0001.

4. If it is a five digit broker, we multiply by 10 to convert it to four digits, and assign this value to the pips variable.

5. If it's a four digits broker and the four digit broker pips is the same as market info view retrieved pips=ticksize. This is an else statement if the first is not true, then we execute this operation else not.

```
 7 #property link       "www.tayyabrashid.com"
 8 #property version    "1.00"
 9 #property strict
10
11 extern double TakeProfit=0.0050;
12 extern double StopLoss=0.0025;
13 extern double LotSize=0.01;
14 double pips=0;        ◄────────────
15 //+----------------------------------------------
16 //| Expert initialization function
17 //+----------------------------------------------
18 int OnInit()
19 {
20 //---
21    PipsFunction();   ◄────────────
22 //---
23    return(INIT_SUCCEEDED);
24 }
25
26 //| Expert deinitialization function
27 //+----------------------------------------------
28 void OnDeinit(const int reason)
29 {
30 //---
31
32 }
33 //+----------------------------------------------
34 //| Expert tick function
35 //+----------------------------------------------
36 void OnTick()
37 {
38    if(IsNewCandle())
39       {
40          if(TotalOpenOrders()<1)
41             {
42                NewOrder();
43             }
44       }
45 }
46 //+
```

10-3 This is how we will use PipsFunction in the script.

You see that the pips variable are defined in the global area because they can be used in several different functions.

We run this function only once therefore we put it in OnInit(). Remember it runs only at the start, so we run it and assign value to our pips variable which we can use in all other variables in the operation. For example, before we begin, our variable pips have no value. When we start the strategy tester, execute the algorithm and when the OnInit() function has been completed it will execute the PipsFunction(); which assigns value to our *pips* variable.

We are building the different functions that we need to manage our trades. What we now need are the following functions: trade, trade execute, lotsize, break-even, and the trailing stop.

11 Break-even function

11.1 Description of the function

Name of The function: BreakEven()

This function will run and check after a predefined distance whether the market has moved in our favor and lock in some pips.

This function will only run if we have an open order, it runs on every tick and not the candle close. We will use the if-statement to check whether there is an open trade, and call this function in tick function if a trade is open. We will have a true/false variable which we put in the OnTick() function to turn breakeven function on/off, and have this variable as changeable in our global area.

Variables in global area:

Extern int MoveToBreakEven=50; This variable we will use to decide after how many pips in our favor that we want to change to break-even.

Extern int PipsProfitLock=20; This variable is used to decide how many pips we want to secure in profit, 0 means break-even and 20 pips means we want to lock in 20 pips of profit.

Extern bool UseBreakeven=true; This variable we use in the tick function, and runs break-even and if this variable is true, it can be changed in the input window.

```
void BreakEven()//1.
{
for(int i=OrdersTotal();i> ;i--)//2.
    {
    if(OrderSelect(i- ,SELECT_BY_POS,MODE_TRADES))//3.
        {
        if(OrderType()==OP_BUY)//4.
            {
            if(Bid-OrderOpenPrice()>MoveToBreakEven*pips)//5.
                {
                if(OrderOpenPrice()>OrderStopLoss())//6.
                    {
                    bool res1=OrderModify(OrderTicket(),OrderOpenPrice(),OrderOpenPrice()+PipsProfit-
Lock*pips,OrderTakeProfit(), ,clrNONE);//7.
                    Alert("Yes");
                    }
                }
            }
        if(OrderType()==OP_SELL)

            {
            if(OrderOpenPrice()-Bid>MoveToBreakEven*pips)
                {
                if(OrderOpenPrice()<OrderStopLoss())
                    {
                    bool res1=OrderModify(OrderTicket(),OrderOpenPrice(),OrderOpenPrice()-Pip-
sProfitLock*pips,OrderTakeProfit(), ,clrNONE);
                    }
                }
            }
        }
    }
}
```

11-1 Breakeven function.

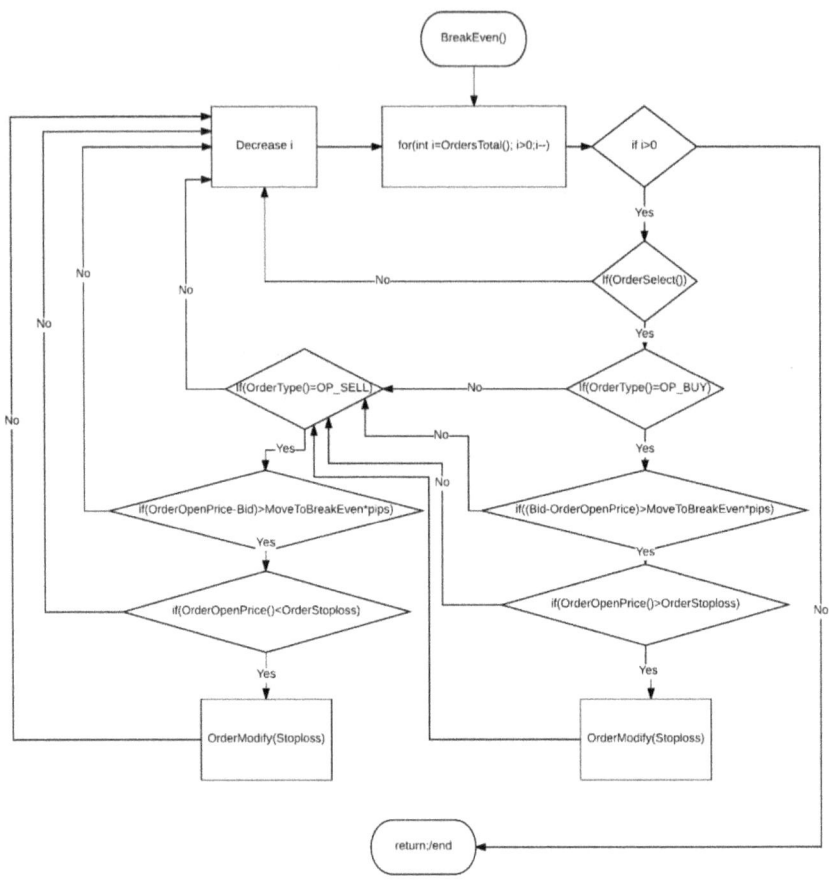

11-2 Flowchart of the BreakEven function.

1. We start by naming the function void BreakEven(), add the open and close brackets and write return before our close bracket.

2. We will use a for loop to loop thru all open orders thru our breakeven function. i equals TotalOrder() and will return current total orders, then begin running the loop thru the

latest order. If there are 8 orders it will begin with the eighth order and decrease order number for every time it has looped thru the function. It will run if i is greater than 0, if i equal 0 it will then pass the control to the end of this function.

3. We use OrderSelect() to select a particular order in our trade pool, as long as there is an order in the pool it will return true else false. If the last decision making passes to OrderSelect() this means there is an order in our trade pool, so this will always be true, and passes control onward after selecting the order.

4. After we have Orderselected() and it has returned true, we check if the selected order is a buy order. If it is a buy order, it will pass the control to the next operation, if not it will run thru the rest of the function which checks if this is a sell order.

5. If it's a buy order the statement will check if the difference(in pips) between current price and order opening price is more than what we have decided in the extern variable MoveToBreakEven . For example if we have set that variable to 40, that variable is not in pips, for us to convert it into pips we multiply with our pips variable which is (0.0001), this will become 0.0040. If the difference is more than 0.0040, the market has moved more than 40 pips in our favor, this will pass the control to the next operation. If it's not true it will then run the same

order thru the sell operation which is also in the function further down.

6. This if statement will check whether the stoploss has already moved by breakeven or trailing function if it has not moved before. This will return true, and it will pass to the next operation. Else pass control to check if it's a sell order and run that operation.

7. Then we use OrderModify() function to execute what we want it to do, everything else is same as the initial order, what we want to change is the stoploss. Since it's a buy order we have to add pips we want to lock in to the OrderOpenPrice(), here again PipsProfitLock is a numeric value like 20 to convert it to pips by multiplying with our pips variable.

8. Then we do the same for the sell side. You see that both orderType() functions are within OrderSelect() function's brackets.

```
10
11 extern int TakeProfit=50;
12 extern int StopLoss=25;
13 extern double LotSize=0.01;
14 double pips;
15 extern int MoveToBreakEven=50;
16 extern int PipsProfitLock=20;
17 extern bool UseBreakEven=True;
18 //+----------------------------------------------
19 //| Expert initialization function
20 //+----------------------------------------------
21 int OnInit()
22   {
23 //---
24   PipsFunction();
25   Alert(pips);
26 //---
27    return(INIT_SUCCEEDED);
28   }
```

11-3 This is how the variable will be in the global area.

In the picture above, we have included variable double pips, we have not assigned any value to it but we have a defined double function. To assign value to it we call on the PipsFunction() at initialization. We have also changed TakeProfit and Stoploss to integer type because instead of 0.0025 we have written 25, on the other side have we multiplied StopLoss and Takeprofit by pips to convert it to 0.0025. We have also used NomalizeDouble() function to convert all to have four decimals in order to round to four decimals.

```
void NewOrder()
{
int Result=OrderSend(Symbol(),OP_BUY,LotSize,Ask, ,NormalizeDouble(Ask-
StopLoss*pips, ),NormalizeDouble(Ask+TakeProfit*pips, ),NULL, , ,clrNONE
);
return;
}
```

11-4 New order function.

11-2 How we use BreakEven Function

We will use it in our Ontick function and before we run the breakeven function we need to check if there is an open order, if there is then it will execute the breakeven function on every tick.

```
void OnTick()
  {
  if(IsNewCandle())
     {
      if(TotalOpenOrders()<1)
          {
          EntrySignal();
          }
      }
     if(TotalOpenOrders()>0)
          {
          if(UseBreakEven)
             {
             BreakEven();
             }
          }
  }
```

11-5 BreakEven function included in the OnTick Function.

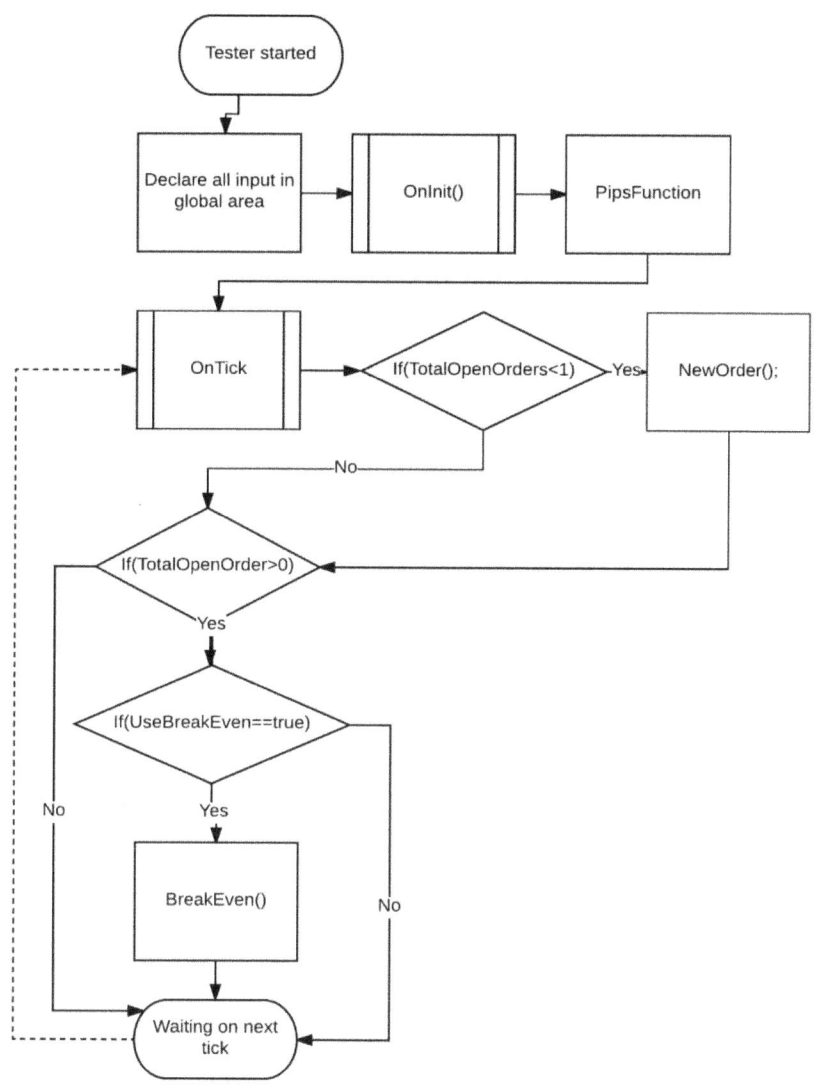

11-6 New flowchart from start to tick function with the BreakEven function included.

You see that in the OnTick() function after executing a trade it will have TotalOpenOrder, if more than one, it passes control to the next if-statement which asks if we have set the UseBreakEven to true, if that's the case it will pass control to the next operation which is running the BreakEven() function.

12 Trailing stop function

12.1 Description of the function

Function name: TrailingStop() this is also a void function.

We want to trail our stoploss in an uptrend, we trail some(distance) pips below the bid, for example 50 pips below the current bid price. After our trailing stop is triggered if the market moves up 50 pips we will change our stop loss 50 pips on the upside.

Variables used in the global area:

Extern bool UseTrailingStop=true; This variable is called on in the tick function, as our BreakEven() function and checks whether we want to use a trailing stop, after the trade has been triggered.

Extern int WhenToTrail=50; We use this variable to see if the market has moved more than this amount of pips when we begin the trailing stop. If we are long and the market has moved in our favor 50 pips we begin trailing the stop loss.

Extern int TrailAmount=50; This variable is what distance we want between our new stop loss and the recent bid price. 50

means we want to trail 50 pips below the recent price. We must multiply both of these with pips to convert these number to pips, 0.0050.

```
void TrailingStop()//1.
{
  for(int i=OrdersTotal();i>0;i--)//2.
    {
    if(OrderSelect(i-1,SELECT_BY_POS,MODE_TRADES))//3.
        {
        if(OrderType()==OP_BUY)//4.
            {
            if(Bid-OrderOpenPrice()>WhenToTrail*pips)//5.
                {
                if(OrderStopLoss()<Bid-TrailAmount*pips)//6.
                    {
                    bool res1=OrderModify(OrderTicket(),OrderOpenPrice(),Bid-
TrailAmount*pips,OrderTakeProfit(),0,clrNONE);//7.
                    }

                }
            }
        if(OrderType()==OP_SELL)
            {
            if(OrderOpenPrice()-Bid>WhenToTrail*pips)
                {
                if(OrderStopLoss()>Bid+TrailAmount*pips)
                    {
                    bool
res1=OrderModify(OrderTicket(),OrderOpenPrice(),Bid+TrailAmount*pips,OrderTakeProfit(),0,clrNO
NE);
                    }
                }
            }
        }

    }
return;
}
```

12-1 Trailingstop function.

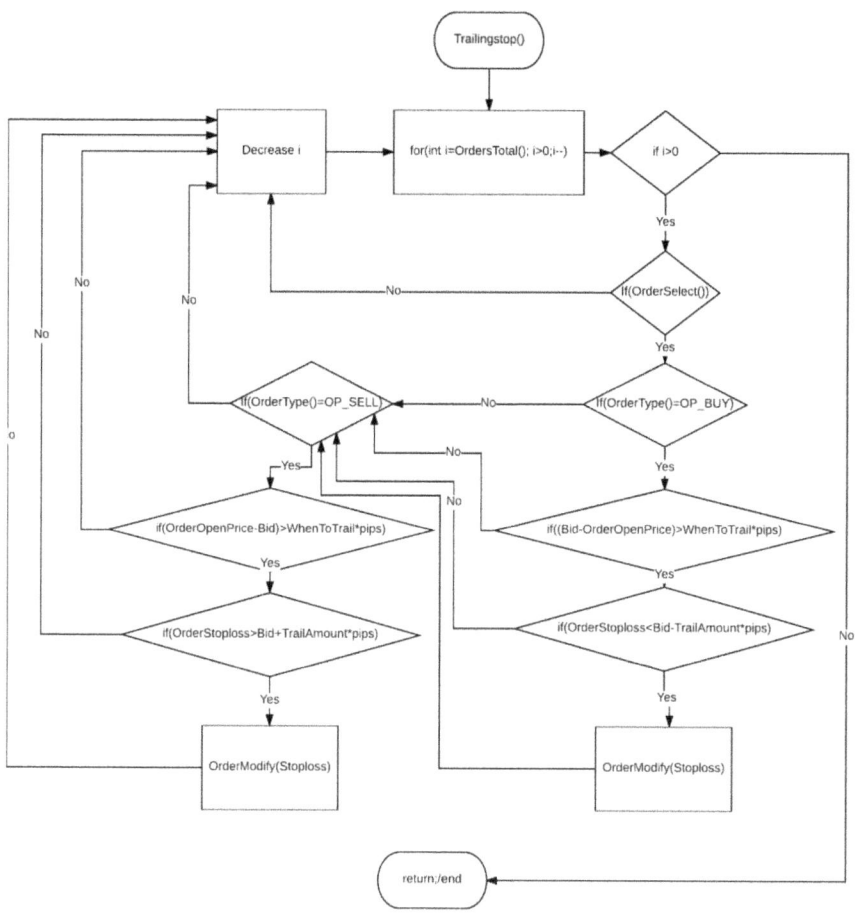

12-2 Flowchart of the TrailingStop() function

1. We start by defining the function void TrailingStop() with an open and closing bracket, and return; before the closing bracket.

2. Here we run all the open orders thru our loop of statements. We use a for loop to do that. Starting with the

latest and decrease *i* for each time the loop has been executed until *i* is zero, then it will pass the control out of this function.

3. We select our order by using OrderSelect() the function has the same input as before. If an order is selected and there is an order in our order pool it will be true. It will have the selected order and pass the operation to the next statement. This will always be yes because if there is no order it will not begin the loop because then TotalOrder() equals 0, which passes control directly out of the loop.

4. With this if-statement operation we check whether the selected order is a buy order, if so, this statement will pass the operation to the next one or else it will run the same order thru the sell operations which are further down, after which it will begin the loop again with the next order.

5. This if-statement checks whether the difference between the current and open price is more than the number of pips we have decided we want to trail after with the WhenToTrail variable. We multiply this variable by pips to convert from 40 to 0.0040. If our variable is 40, the market has moved more than 40 pips in our favor, this statement will pass the operation to the next statement or else it will pass control to check if this is a sell order.

6. This checks if this is a buy order, if our current stop loss is less then where we want to trail. If orderstoploss is 1.4500

and we want the trail stop loss to be at 1.4505 then this statement will become true and pass operation to the next statement, meaning we must change the stop loss to where we want to trail. Otherwise it will pass control to check if this is a sell order and run thru the remainder of those operations.

7. We Use OrderModify() function to change stoploss behind the bid price we want stoploss to trail, we also use pips to convert TrailAmount to pips.

Declaration of variables in Global Area:

```
extern int TakeProfit=50;
extern int StopLoss=25;
extern double LotSize=0.01;

double pips;

extern bool UseBreakEven=True;
extern int MoveToBreakEven=50;
extern int PipsProfitLock=20;

extern bool UseTrailingStop=true;
extern int WhenToTrail=50;
extern int TrailAmount=30;
```

12-3 This is the global variable area with the trailingstop function.

12-2 How to use TrailingStop

As a BreakEven() function this will also be placed in our OnTick function after TotalOpenOrders>0 if- statements.

```
void OnTick()
 {
 if(IsNewCandle())
    {
     if(TotalOpenOrders()< )
        {
         EntrySignal();
        }
    }
    if(TotalOpenOrders()> )
        {
         if(UseBreakEven)
            {
             BreakEven();
            }
         if(UseTrailingStop)
            {
             TrailingStop();
            }
        }
 }
```

12-4 This is the OnTick() function when you include the TrailingStop function.

As with the BreakEven() function we include this function in the same brackets, within brackets of the if-statement checking if there is an open order. If orders are open it will check if we have set Usebreakeven to true, if that's true it will run the breakeven function. It then checks if we have set UseTrailingStop to true, if that's the case it will run the Trailingstop function. If we have no open orders it will go to the end of the program.

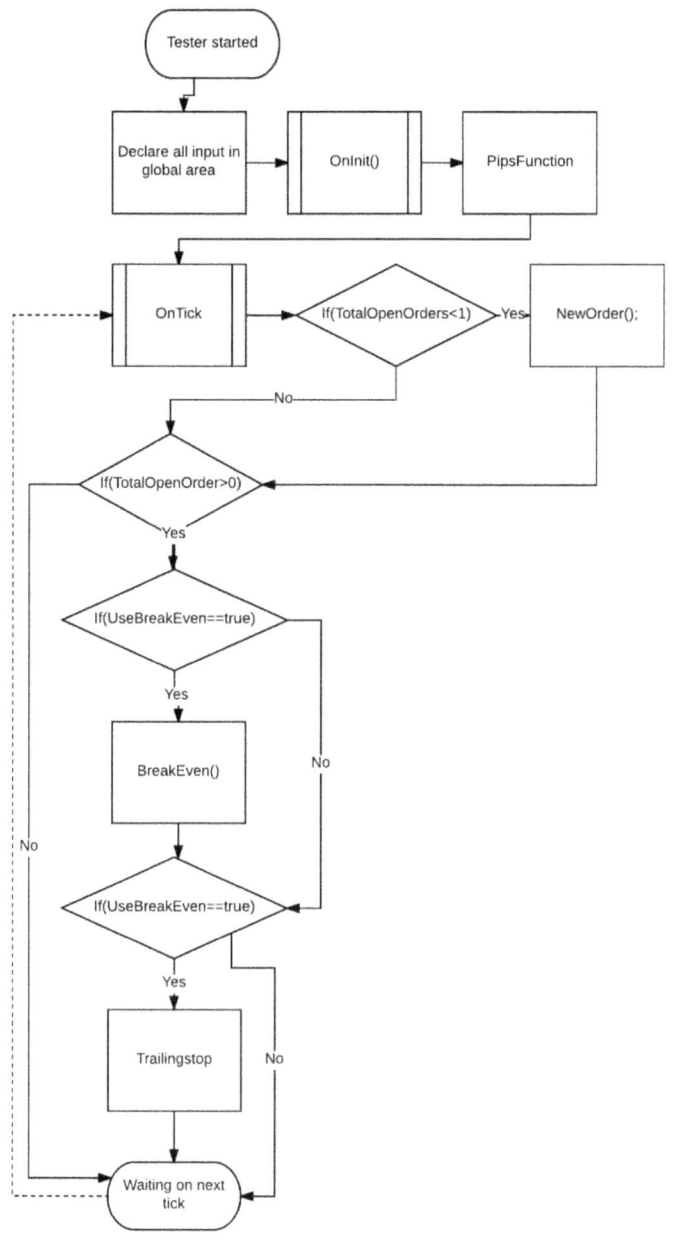

12-5 Flowchart of the Ontick() function with the TrailingStop included

13 Trade function

13.1 Description of the function

We have been making functions, the most important is the trade sending function, which includes the option to turn stoploss and takeprofit off, set takeprofit as a function of stoploss(risk/reward) and the option to positionsize.

Function name will be: Trade(int direction)

Int direction is an input parameter which we will use to call if we want to trade a buy or sell order.

Trade(0) for buyorder and Trade(1) for sellorder.

We will have the option to have a stop loss or no stop loss.

We will have the option to have a take profit or no take profit.

We will have a position with a risk/reward ratio, for this we need the stop loss turned on.

We will have automated position sizing, this needs the stop loss turned on and be able to choose risk percent per trade.

Variable in Global Area:

extern bool UseStoploss=true; This will be true if want to use stop loss and false if not

extern bool UseTakeProfit=true; This will be true if we want to use takeprofit, false if not

extern bool UsePosition=true; This will be true if we want to use positionsizing, false if not

extern bool UseRiskReward=true; This will be true if we want to use Risk/reward ratio

extern double reward_ratio=2; This is the risk reward ratio, if it's true this means takeprofit is double of stoploss

extern int RiskPercent=1; This is positionsizing percent how many percent of our current equity do we want to trade on each trade, our risk on each trade.

Call on the function:

This function will be called by a trade Logic function which we will define by Trade(0) or Trade(1).

```
void Trade(int Direction)//1.
{
double SL;//2.
double TP;//3.
double Equity=AccountEquity();//4
double RiskedAmount=Equity*RiskPercent*0.01;//5.
double Lots=0;//6.
   if(Direction==0)//.7
   {
   if(UseStoploss)//8.
        {
        SL=Bid-StopLoss*pips;
        }
        else
        {
        SL=0;
        }
     double PipsToBuyStoploss=StopLoss*pips;
     if(UseTakeProfit)//.9
        {
        if(UseRiskReward && UseStoploss)//10.
           {
           TP=(Bid-SL)*2+Bid;
           }
        else
           {
           TP=Bid+TakeProfit*pips;
           }
        }
        else
        {
        TP=0;
        }
     if(UsePosition && UseStoploss)//.11
     {
      Lots=(RiskedAmount/(PipsToBuyStoploss/pips))/10;
     }
     else
     {
     Lots=LotSize;
     }
     int res=OrderSend(Symbol(),OP_BUY,Lots,Ask,3,NormalizeDou-
ble(SL,4),NormalizeDouble(TP,4),NULL,0,0,clrNONE);//11.
   }
   if(Direction==1)
   {
     if(UseStoploss)
        {
        SL=Ask+StopLoss*pips;
        }
        else
        {
        SL=0;
        }
     double PipsToSellStoploss=StopLoss*pips;
     if(UseTakeProfit)
        {
        if(UseRiskReward && UseStoploss)
           {
           TP=Ask-((SL-Ask)*2);
           }
```

13-1 Trade() function.

96

1. This function is a void function. We write void Trade(int direction), open and closing brackets and return before the closing bracket to tell the executor that this is the end of this function and the control will be given outside the function from there. Direction is an input variable that will be used to call on the function, it's an integer type. It will be called like Trade(0) for buy order and Trade(1) for sell order, 0 1 is integer type therefore variable Direction is a integer type.

2. We are defining a new double variable SL(stop loss) which we will use to place in our OrderSend() function with no initial value assigned to it.

3. We are defining new double variable TP(take profit) which we will use to place in our OrderSend() function with no initial value assigned.

4. We have a double function named equity, this variable will be assigned the current account value

5. We have a double variable named risked amount, this is the amount we want to risk on a particular trade. We multiply current equity with the risk we want to put on this trade with RiskPercent variable in our global area, because it's integer type and we want to convert it to percent we multiply this with 0.01

6. We have a variable called Lots, with zero initial value assigned. All these variables are local variables, they can only be used within this function.

7. When calling on the function we have called in This was Trade(0) it will run everything within this statement bracket.

8. First thing is to decide the stop loss, if UseStoploss is equal to stoploss is Bid-Stoploss*pips else is equal to zero.

9. We decide the stop loss. If stoploss is equal to true then we have to ask whether we are using risk to reward(is this true).

10. If this is true takeprofit is for example two times stoploss if it's not true stoploss is Bid+TakeProfit*pips.

11. Then we must see if UsePosition and stoploss are equal to true, if so then lotsize is a function of Riskedamount and our stoploss.

12. We place our trade with all the input variables we have selected from the beginning in the function.

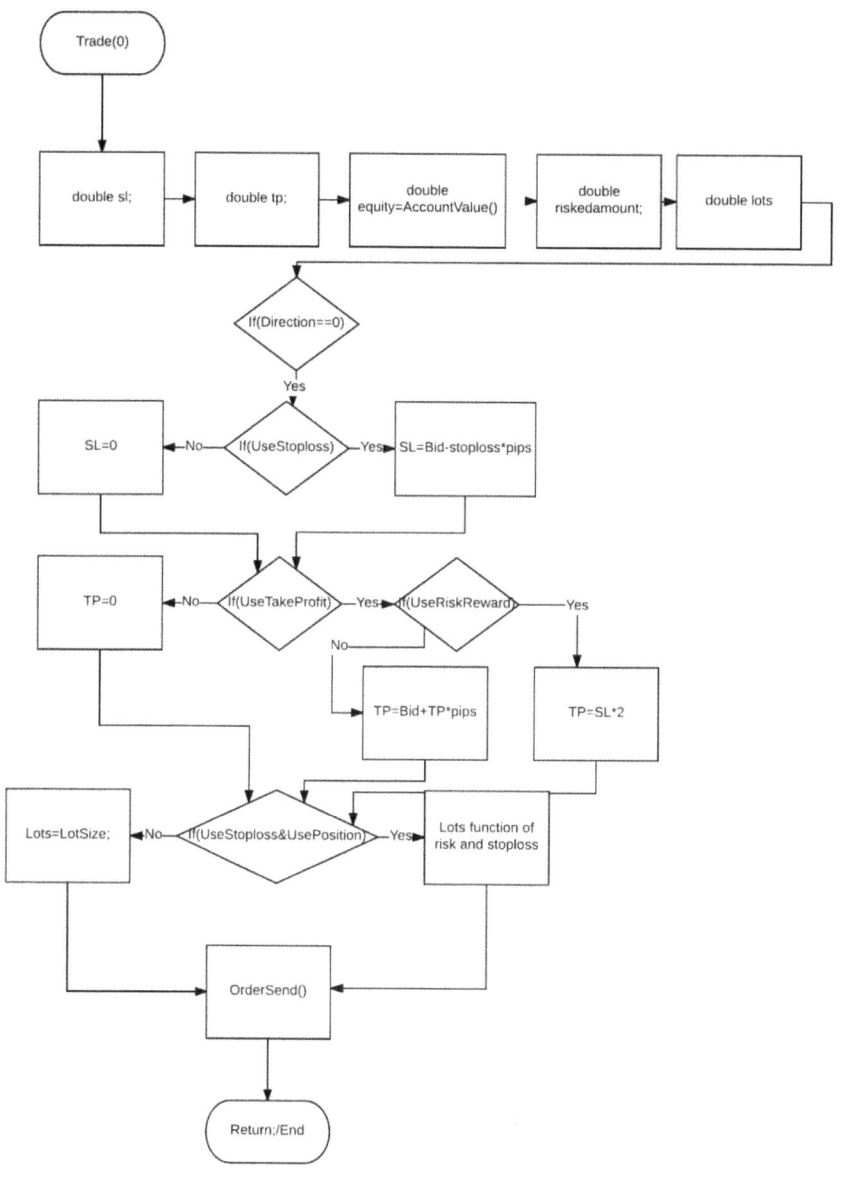

13-2 Flowchart of Trade() function.

We call on Trade(0) function which checks for If Direction is equal to zero, indicating the input function is equal to zero. If that is true it will run thru everything stated between the opening and closing brackets of if(Direction==0) statement and will run everything we have stated in the flowchart above.

```
10
11 extern int TakeProfit=50;
12 extern int StopLoss=25;
13 extern double LotSize=0.01;
14
15 double pips;
16
17 extern bool UseBreakEven=True;
18 extern int MoveToBreakEven=50;
19 extern int PipsProfitLock=20;
20
21 extern bool UseTrailingStop=true;
22 extern int WhenToTrail=50;
23 extern int TrailAmount=30;
24 extern bool UseStoploss=true;
25 extern bool UseTakeProfit=true;
26 extern bool UsePosition=true;
27 extern bool UseRiskReward=true;
28 extern double reward_ratio=2;
29 extern int RiskPercent=1;
30
31
```

13-3 Above you see how our global area looks.

13.2 How to use Trade()

We will use this function later, when we make a function Strategy() where we write trade logic and from that call on this Trade() function.

14 CandleClose function

14.1 Function description

There are different ways to close a trade, some traders close with a stop loss and take profit, others use close after some candle rule. We create this function because we also need it to create a strategy.

Function name: CandleClose();

Variables in Global area:

extern Bool UseCandleClose=true; This variable is placed in the global area and is an extern variable because we need it to be changeable. If we want to use CandleClose() we set it to true or false.

extern int CloseAfterCandles=1; This is an integer variable and will decide after how many candles do we want to close our order. 1 means we want to close this trade after one candle trade has been executed.

Where to apply the function: The function should run on every tick if one order is open. It is placed within the same bracket as our BreakEven and TrailingStop function.

Variables in Local area:

Int period=Period(); This variable is assigned function Period(), period returns the value of which time period we are running this algo on. If we are running one minute chart it will return 1, and 5 if we are running five minute, 60 if are running on hourly and 240 if we are running on 4 hour which is 1 hour*4=60*4=240.

int period2=0; This variable has initially a value of zero because by using a switch function we want to assign a value to it. This variable will return timeframe seconds. For example if it's attached to one minute, there are 60 seconds in one minute, so then period2 has value of 60. If it is attached to 1 hour chart there are 60*60=3600 seconds in one hour so this variable will get a value of 3600, but this is done by using a switch function.

```
void CandleClose()//1
{
    int period=Period();//2.
    int period2= ;//3.


    switch(period)//4.
    {   case  :period2=  ;break;
        case  :period2=   ;break;
        case   :period2=   ;break;
        case   :period2=    ;break;
        case   :period2=    ;break;
        case    :period2=     ;break;
        case     :period2=     ;break;
        case      :period2=      ;break;
        case      :period2=       ;break;
        //default: Alert("Nothing");
    }

for(int i=OrdersTotal();i>  ;i--)//5.
    {
    if(OrderSelect(i- ,SELECT_BY_POS,MODE_TRADES))//6.
        {
        if(TimeCurrent()-OrderOpenTime()>period2*CloseAfterCandles)//7.
            {
            CloseAllOrders();//8.
            }
        }
    }
    return;
}
```

14-1 The CloseCandle() Function

1. We begin writing the type of function which is void. Then
   we name the function which is *CancleClose* and write
   opening and closing parentheses after the function name
   to alert the system that this is a function. Next we need an
   opening and a closing bracket which has all the operations
   within the function. Before the closing bracket we need to

write *return;* to indicate that this is the end of the function and control is be passed out of the function to the next operation, either it is executing the next function or ending.

2. We have to define our variable period as an integer, and assign value Period() which will return the timeframe this algo is running on. If it's one minute timeframe it will return 1 and 60 if its hourly, and 240 if it's 4 hour timeframe.

3. This is our next variable in local area, variable which can only be used within this function. This variable is an integer, and initially we assign a value of 0, but it will be given a value after we have run the switch operation which is next in the function. The name of this function is *period2*.

4. This is a switch operator, it's the same as an if-statement but with more cases. You begin by writing switch with opening and closing parentheses, in the parentheses you write the name of the variable you want to check. Until now *period* would have been given a value return by the *period()* function. Then you add an open and closing brackets to state all the cases. We have a number if that *period* has been assigned value 1, we will assign a value of 60 to variable period2 because it is 60 seconds in one minute. If that's the case after assigning the value we have written *break;* what this operator does is instead of that

after assigning value *period2* and case is *period 1* it will not check the rest of the cases and pass the control out of the switch operator brackets to the next operation in the function. This way we save some time, but if we don't write break; it will continue to check whether case is 5,15 and so on. We have assigned a value to all variables that we need in the future operations both variables *period* and *period2*

5. Then we have a for loop which will run thru all open orders, starting with the latest order and decrease one by one.

6. We need to select an order in our trade pool to check the trade in the next operation.

7. Here we have an if-statement meaning decision statement. Function TimeCurrent() returns second current seconds since 1970, the number of seconds since 1970. OrderOpenTime() returns how many seconds have passed since 1970 when we execute the trade. The difference between these two is how many seconds the trade has been open. Period2 has the value we have assigned it using the switch operator. If we are running this strategy on a hourly chart, *period2* has a value of 3600(number of seconds in one hour) and we multiply this by the number of candles or hours after we want to close. 1 if we want to close after one hour and 2 etc if want to close this trade after two hourly candles(two hours). This

if statement checks when the trade duration time in seconds is more than value on the right side of > if that's the case then it passes the control to the next operation.

8. Next operation is calling on our function CloseAllOrder(); which we already have built and is in the same script. It closes all open orders and delete pending orders.

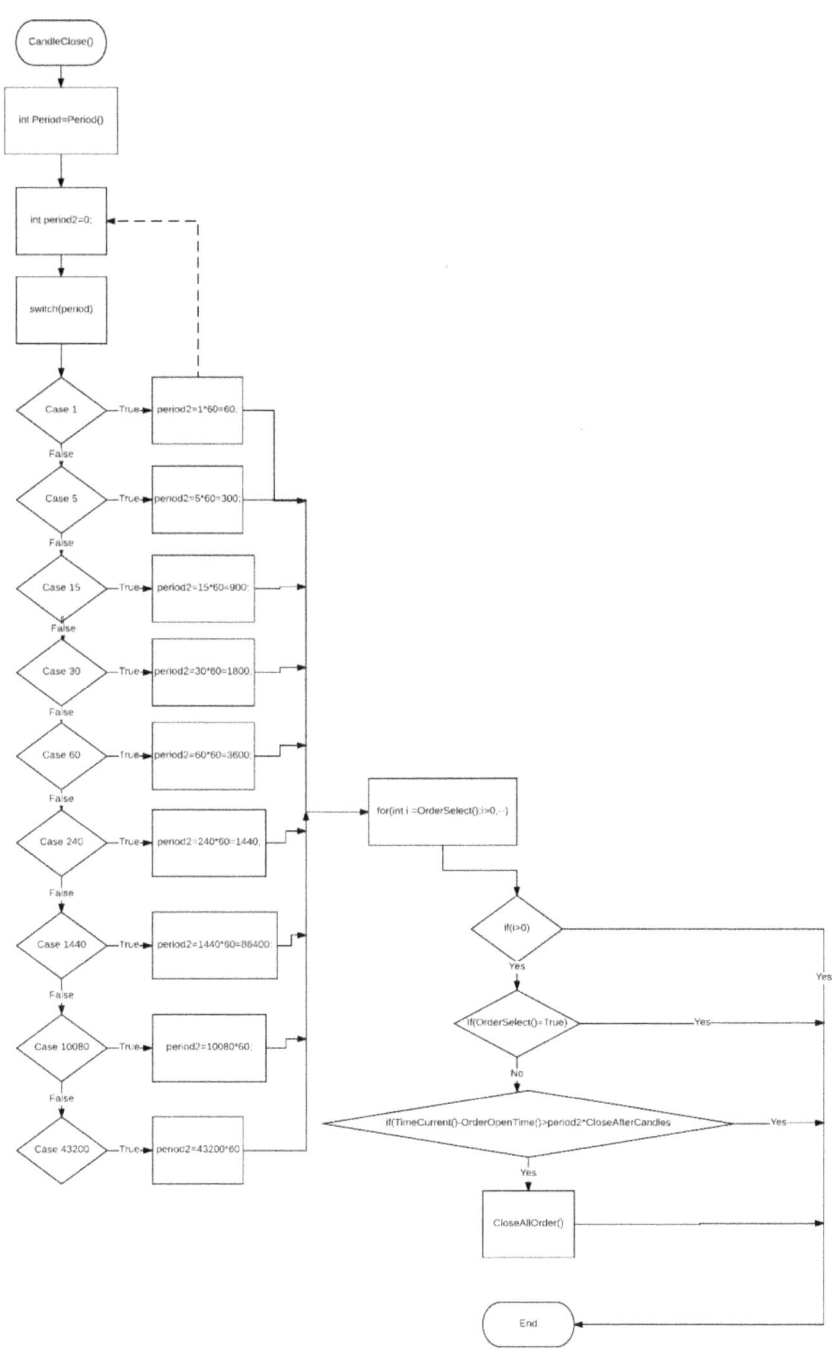

14-2 Flowchart of the CloseCandle() function.

```
11 extern int TakeProfit=50;
12 extern int StopLoss=25;
13 extern double LotSize=0.01;
14
15 double pips;
16
17 extern bool UseBreakEven=True;
18 extern int MoveToBreakEven=50;
19 extern int PipsProfitLock=20;
20
21 extern bool UseTrailingStop=true;
22 extern int WhenToTrail=50;
23 extern int TrailAmount=30;
24 extern bool UseStoploss=true;
25 extern bool UseTakeProfit=true;
26 extern bool UsePosition=true;
27 extern bool UseRiskReward=true;
28 extern double reward_ratio=2;
29 extern int RiskPercent=1;
30 extern bool UseCandleClose=true;
31 extern int CloseAfterCandles=1;
```

14-3 This is the global variable with CandleClose() function.

14.2 How to use CandleClose function

Now we have built a function which we will use to design our trading strategy. We must set UseCandleClose=true; and decide the candle number we want to close after in the global area. When we are using this function you must set UseStopLoss and UseTakeProfit as false otherwise you will get two closing mechanisms.

```
void OnTick()
  {
  if(IsNewCandle())
     {
      if(TotalOpenOrders()< )
          {
          EntrySignal();
          }
     }
     if(TotalOpenOrders()> )
          {
          if(UseBreakEven)
             {
             BreakEven();
             }
          if(UseTrailingStop)
             {
             TrailingStop();
             }
           if(UseCandleClose)
             {
             CandleClose();
             }
          }
  }
```

14-4 This is the OnTick() function with the candle close function included.

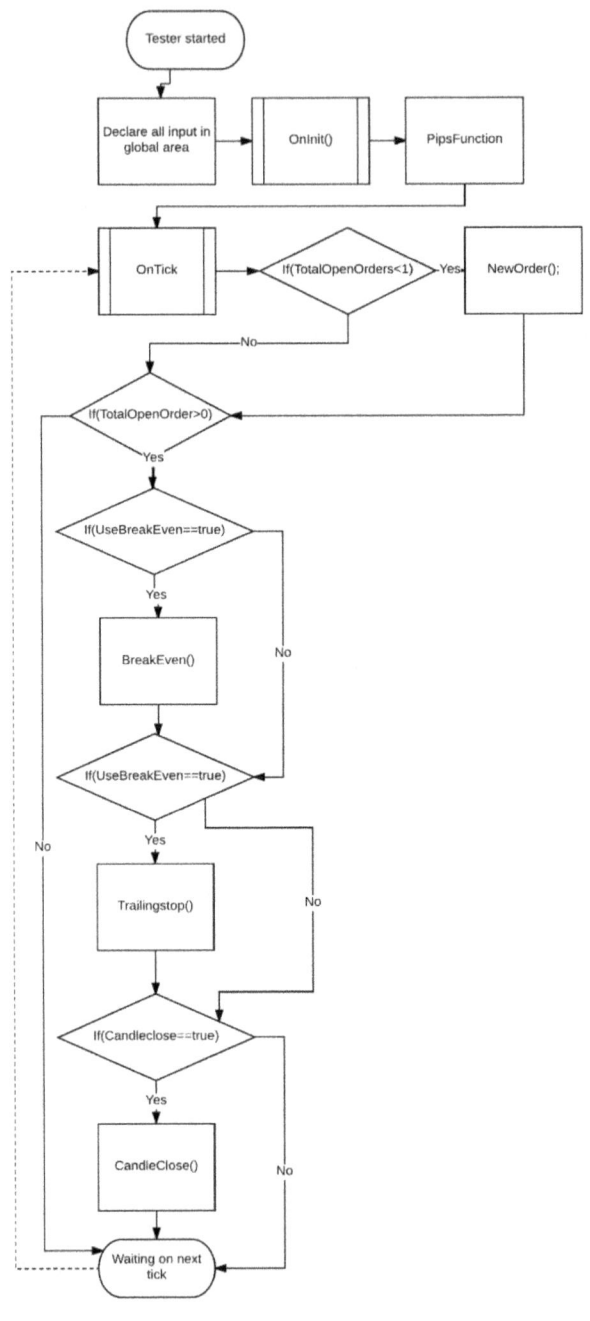

14-5 The flowchart for Ontick() function with Candleclose().

15 Strategy function

15.1 Function description

This is the function where we decide on our strategy. We call on function Trade(0) for a buy order and Trade(1) for a sell order.

Function name: EntrySignal()

Variables in the Global Area:

Extern int ShortMAPeriod=50; This is the input to the moving average function of Shorter term and how many periods we are using of shorter term.

Extern int LongMAPeriod=100; This is the input to the moving average function of longer term, as moving average periods.

extern bool TradeLong=true; This variable is true if we want to trade long in our strategy.

extern bool TradeShort=true; This variable is true if we want to trade short in our strategy.

Variables in Functions Local Area:

We need to calculate the different moving averages. Because we are going to trade on crossovers we need to calculate one period and two periods prior moving averages. For the long trade the two periods prior short term moving average should be below the long term moving average and the one period prior, the short term should be above the long term and then we have a crossover strategy.

```
double
ShortMaCurrent=iMA(Symbol(),PERIOD_CURRENT,ShortMAPeriod,0,MODE_SMA,PRICE_CLOSE,1);

double
LongMaCurrent=iMA(Symbol(),PERIOD_CURRENT,LongMAPeriod,0,MODE_SMA,PRICE_CLOSE,1);

double
ShortMaPrevious=iMA(Symbol(),PERIOD_CURRENT,ShortMAPeriod,0,MODE_SMA,PRICE_CLOSE,2);

double
LongMaPrevious=iMA(Symbol(),PERIOD_CURRENT,LongMAPeriod,0,MODE_SMA,PRICE_CLOSE,2);
```

You see that global variables which are changeable are the input in the local variables.

```
void EntrySignal()//0
{
double
ShortMaCurrent=iMA(Symbol(),PERIOD_CURRENT,ShortMAPeriod, ,MODE_SMA,PRICE_C
LOSE, );//1.
double
LongMaCurrent=iMA(Symbol(),PERIOD_CURRENT,LongMAPeriod, ,MODE_SMA,PRICE_CLO
SE, );
double
ShortMaPrevious=iMA(Symbol(),PERIOD_CURRENT,ShortMAPeriod, ,MODE_SMA,PRICE_
CLOSE, );
double
LongMaPrevious=iMA(Symbol(),PERIOD_CURRENT,LongMAPeriod, ,MODE_SMA,PRICE_CL
OSE, );

    if(TradeLong)//.2
    {
        if(ShortMaPrevious<LongMaPrevious &&
ShortMaCurrent>LongMaCurrent)//3.
        {
        Trade( );//.4
        }
    }
    if(TradeShort)
    {
        if(ShortMaPrevious>LongMaPrevious && ShortMaCurrent<LongMaCurrent)
        {
        Trade( );
        }
    }
return;
}
```

15-1 This how our strategy function will appear with the moving average crossover.

0. We begin by writing void because this function only executes what is stated within its brackets, then the function name with open and closing parentheses. We then add an opening and closing bracket with *return;* in it.

1. We write the local variables we will use in this function and see that local variables have global extern variables as input variables.

2. We check if we have set our TradeLong bool variable to true or false, if it's true it passes control to the next operation.

3. This is also an if-statement which checks if the two period short moving average was below the slow moving average and one period fast moving average is above one period slow moving average meaning checks for a cross. If the cross has happened then it will call on the function Trade() with 0 input variable which means buy orders.

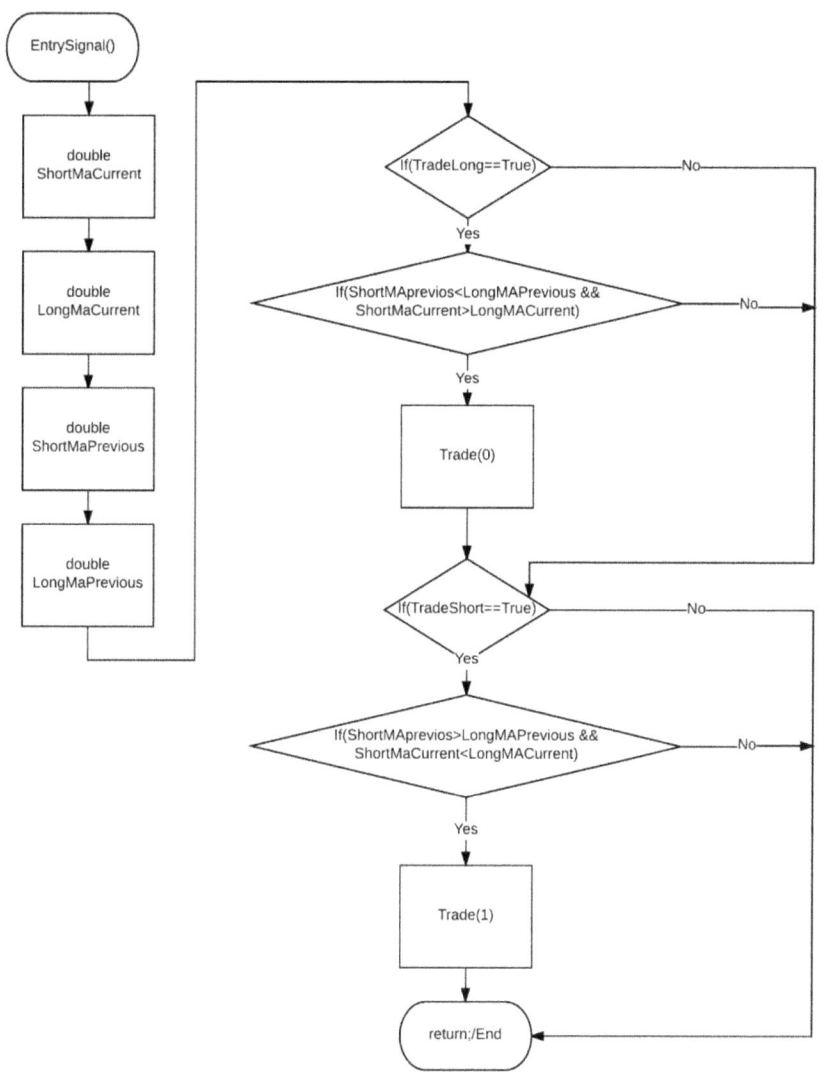

15-2 Flowchart of the Entry Signal

```
 1 //+--------------------------------------------------------------+
 2 //|                                              MyAlgo.mq4    |
 3 //|                                              Tayyab Rashid |
 4 //|                                       www.tayyabrashid.com |
 5 //+--------------------------------------------------------------+
 6 #property copyright "Tayyab Rashid"
 7 #property link      "www.tayyabrashid.com"
 8 #property version   "1.00"
 9 #property strict
10
11 extern int TakeProfit=50;
12 extern int StopLoss=25;
13 extern double LotSize=0.01;
14
15 double pips;
16
17 extern bool UseBreakEven=True;
18 extern int MoveToBreakEven=50;
19 extern int PipsProfitLock=20;
20
21 extern bool UseTrailingStop=true;
22 extern int WhenToTrail=50;
23 extern int TrailAmount=30;
24 extern bool UseStoploss=true;
25 extern bool UseTakeProfit=true;
26 extern bool UsePosition=true;
27 extern bool UseRiskReward=true;
28 extern double reward_ratio=2;
29 extern int RiskPercent=1;
30 extern bool UseCandleClose=true;
31 extern int CloseAfterCandles=1;
32 extern bool TradeLong=true;
33 extern bool TradeShort=true;
34 extern int ShortMAPeriod=50;
35 extern int LongMAPeriod=100;
36
```

15-3 This is the variable in the global area with all the functions
included also EntrySignal().

16 How to use this function

We will place the EntrySignal() in our Ontick function and within the brackets of IsNewCandle() and TotalOpenOrders<1 if-statement.

```
void OnTick()
  {
  if(IsNewCandle())
     {
      if(TotalOpenOrders()< )
         {
         EntrySignal();
         }
     }
     if(TotalOpenOrders()> )
         {
         if(UseBreakEven)
            {
            BreakEven();
            }
         if(UseTrailingStop)
            {
            TrailingStop();
            }
          if(UseCandleClose)
            {
            CandleClose();
            }
         }
  }
```

16-1 This is the OnTick() function with EntrySignal() function included.

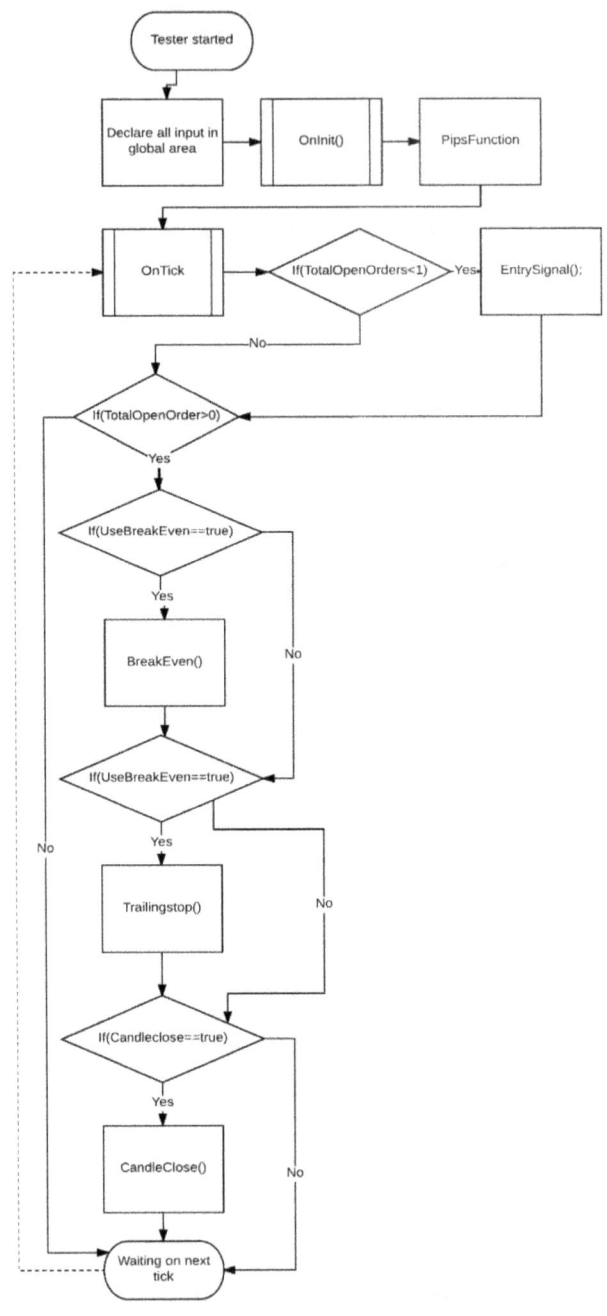

16-2 Flowchart with EntrySignal() function included.

17 Designing a trading strategy

First, ask yourself why do you want to trade. As long as you are in the market your capital is at risk. You can take big risks to make big rewards which equals gambling techniques, or you can trade wisely and control your risk to make reasonable profits in the long term. Professional traders make yearly approx. 7%, on average, a drawdown which is acceptable is double of your return.

You now have the building blocks that you can use along with the freedom to adjust them and they will still remain effective. To avoid curve fitting, you need a system that includes volatility parameters but you must not over optimize or optimize several different parameters at once.

Trading strategy development

1. Find an entry signal, this is accomplished by changing the EntrySignal() function and put your own trading logic and set CandleClose()(Stoploss, Takeprofit, Breakeven and Trailing function to false because we will not use any of them). Close the position after 5-10-20-30 candles and see which type of entry signal it is, it should generate a

positive overall return. Then it's worth going further with this trading signal.

2. Remember to have a significant test time period, plus include many types of markets, uptrend, downtrend and ranging markets. Volatile uptrend, average volatility uptrend and excess volatility, are also included in your test. Run the same entry logic on different pairs and different timeframes to find out which one is best. You will quickly understand that a breakout entry will have a positive overall return when you use candle close and choose to close just after 5-10 candles, but a trend strategy will need more time to be in profit. So based on your trading strategy you should be able to narrow your close after a number of candles parameter. Often there is not the same open and closing mechanism for long and short trades, so you might first find a strategy for long and then one for short.

3. When you have chosen the timeframe and a good performing pair. You try to combine your entry strategy with different exit strategies. It could be a dynamic stop-loss and take-profit, trailing stop, 60 period simple moving average trailing stop, with or without breakeven. You should have predefined rules.

4. To be successful you need a diversified portfolio of strategies on different pairs and timeframes. Because if you have a trend strategy it will lose money in ranging

market but if you also have a strategy for ranging markets you will make money on that.

5. Whatever system you have, return to drawdown ratio can be as large as 1:2.

6. Sometimes it might be best to go the other way around and design an exit system(what you want from the market), and then design a entry signal.

17.1 If-Statement

This is frequently used in functions and it is decision making, or in other words we ask the question whether a statement is true or not.

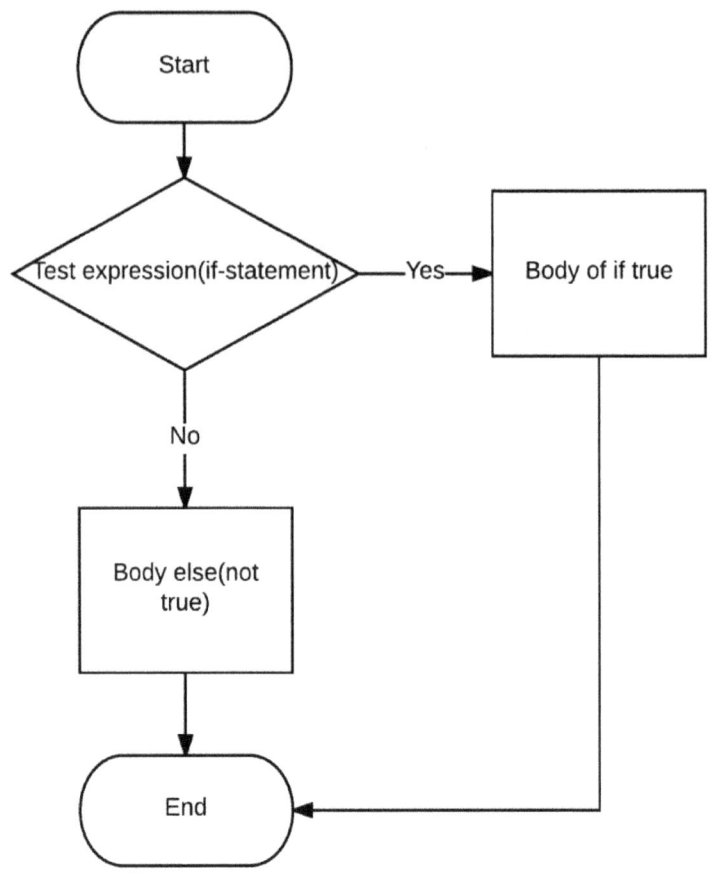

This is a flow chart of an if-statement.

From start, pass the control to if-statement. If the statement is true then everything in the *Body of true* is executed. But if that's not the case and the statement is not true but false, then everything in body else will be executed, and both will pass control to the *end*.

Code: Binary Extra, Redeem at www.gcmsonline.info at contact us.

Example 1:

```
void Test1()
{
    int A= ;
    int B= ;
    if(A>B)
    {
        Comment("A is bigger Than B");
    }
    else
    {
        Comment("A is less than B");
    }
return;
}
```

This is an example of an if-statement, we have a function called Test1. It starts with defining two variables A and B.

Then we have an if-statement which ask whether A is bigger than B. Then if that's true we have an output comment which is "A is bigger than B". If the statement is false, A is less than B, then we have else body which will be executed. A comment "A is less than B".

Example 2:

```
void Test2()
{
    int A= ;
    int B= ;
    if(A>B)
    {
        Comment("A is bigger Than B");
    }
return;
```

This is another type of using if-statement, it checks whether the statement is true, if it is true it will comment "A is bigger Than B" if it is not true it will just pass the control to the end. You can see the flowchart of it below.

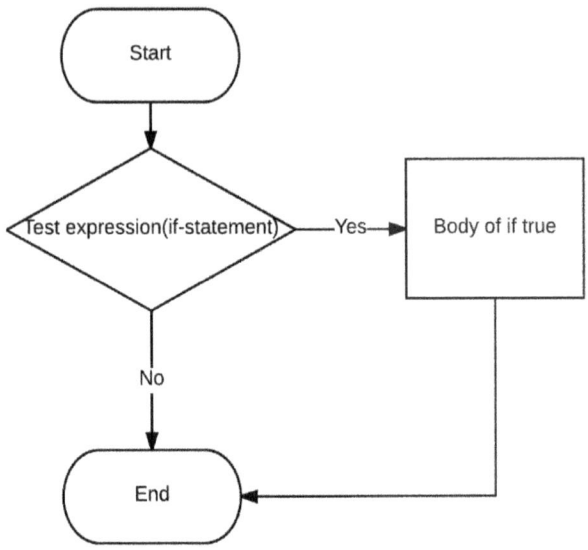

If-statement without else statements.

17.2 For loop function

You can use for or while loop. We use a for loop.

Example of for loop:

```
void test2()
{
    int Number= ;
    for(int i= ;i> ;i--)
    {
        Number=Number+ ;
    }
}
```

Example on a for loop

Here we have a function called test2, which begins by declaring a variable Number as integer and assigning value of zero. Then we run a for loop.

We start by writing for and two parentheses as a function with an opening and closing bracket. In the parentheses, we write three variables. First variable is how many times we want to run this function or loop which we will define between the opening and closing bracket, it will execute everything between them each loop. The second variable is how long do we want to loop, as long as i is more than zero. The third variable defined which is either style ascending or descending. ++ means it will start with number one and then loop 2 and 3. - - means it will start with 3 then loop 2 and 1, and stop there because we want to loop as long as i is above 0. In the opening and closing brackets we write everything we want to execute on each loop.

Below is the flowchart of the loop above.

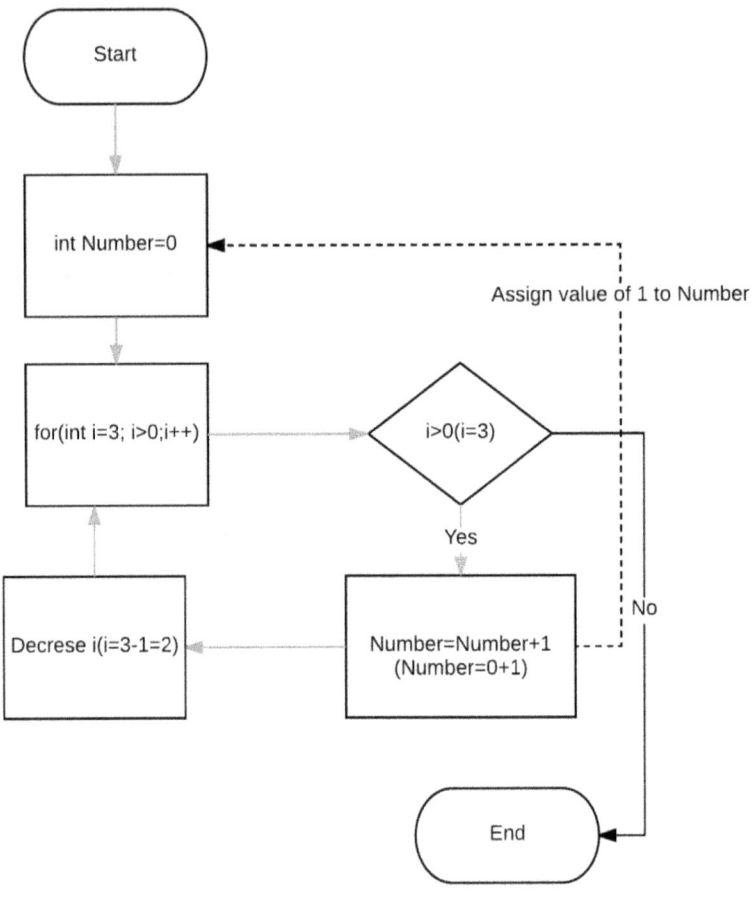

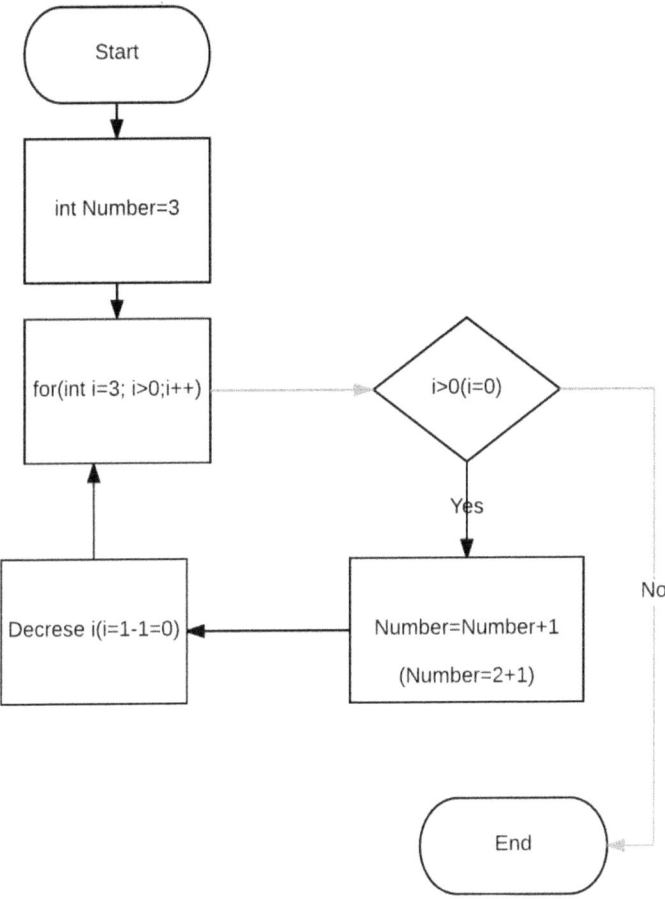

If you found this book useful in any way, a review on Amazon is always appreciated!

www.ingramcontent.com/pod-product-compliance
Lightning Source LLC
Chambersburg PA
CBHW061440180526
45170CB00004B/1492